REACHING INTIMACY
A Male Sex Surrogate's Perspective

JERRY DE HAAN

REACHING INTIMACY

A Male Sex Surrogate's Perspective

ST. MARTIN'S PRESS · NEW YORK

Design by Victoria Hartman

Library of Congress Cataloging in Publication Data

DeHaan, Jerry.
    Reaching intimacy.

    1. DeHaan, Jerry.   2. Sex surrogates—California—
Biography.   I. Title.
RC557.5.S94D44   1986   616.85′83206 [B]   85-27870
ISBN 0-312-66434-6

First Edition

10 9 8 7 6 5 4 3 2 1

Contents

Acknowledgments

As a surrogate, I recognize that I am indebted to a long list of people who have been instrumental in making me effective and successful in my work. Barbara Roberts, a sex therapist, was a powerful influence on my life. Through her encouragement and training, I evolved from a confused man into a confident and competent surrogate. My mentors, Dr. Jack Spund and Adele Kennedy, contributed their guidance and their confidence in my potential, thus helping me grow. And every therapist with whom I have worked has advanced my development through wise counseling and sound advice. I thank all of these good friends and co-workers for the invaluable contributions they have made to my life.

I must also take this opportunity to thank my clients, each of whom, in the course of her own therapy, has given me confidence and love. Without their determination to overcome problems, my work would have been in vain.

As a writer, I have yet another list of people to whom I am indebted. I have always wanted to be a writer, but it wasn't until I began to put together the notes for this book that I realized how much hard labor goes into acquiring that title. Several people attempted to help me organize my notes—but to no avail. I knew I needed help, but just anyone wouldn't do. I needed someone who could comprehend my work and what I was trying to say. Such a person appeared in the form of two writers—the team of Iris and Keith Bancroft. Although neither of them is a surrogate or therapist, they are the only people I know outside of that select circle who understand me and have the skills to put my jumbled thoughts in order. I thank them for their work.

I also thank Sandy Watt, my agent, who never gave up, even when I was in despair and convinced that what I had to say would never reach public view. It was her tenacity, as much as my notes and the Bancrofts' writing, that finally brought this book into being.

I must also give credit and thanks to my children—Christine, herself a psychologist, who lent her support and expertise, and Bradley, whose counsel and guidance helped greatly—for their unqualified loving, caring, and encouragement.

Last, and to me most important, I thank my wife, Rose, for her wonderful love and understanding. Without her by my side, my failures would bring me to despair, and my triumphs would lose their joy.

J.D.

REACHING INTIMACY
A Male Sex Surrogate's Perspective

1

AN AWAKENING
The Power of Vulnerability

I was introduced to Emma in the therapist's office. She had an alert manner and seemed to be interested in everything that was happening. As I met her steady gaze, I found her unexpectedly appealing. I couldn't believe she was coming to me as a client. While we conversed quietly with the therapist, I realized she was watching me warily. I fervently hoped she couldn't see my nervousness.

I was, at first, puzzled by my reactions. I wasn't supposed to feel nervous. After all, I was a graduate of a bona fide school for surrogates. Nor was I supposed to feel any unprofessional reaction to a client. But here I was, assessing this woman as I would a possible date. She certainly wasn't my choice as far as looks went—and I suspected that I was not hers either. Nevertheless, I felt an attraction—to her bright awareness, to her quick wit. As we continued to talk, both the nervousness and the attraction remained.

At last, alone for the first time, we stood facing each other, smiling. "Are you always so uneasy with a client?" She wasn't condemning—just curious.

2. REACHING INTIMACY

Even before I answered, I felt better. There was a lilt to her voice that put me at ease. She didn't know she was my first client, but she had instinctively broken the tension—a job that should have fallen to me.

"A little." I felt an urge to smile. "I'm concerned that we get along well. I can help more that way. And I'm hoping we'll find some common ground, so neither of us will be uncomfortable."

Incredible though it seemed, her smile became even brighter than before. "I think we've crossed that hurdle. Don't you?"

That was the easy part, I learned.

As we spoke together, I mentally reviewed what I knew of Emma's history. She had had a very traditional upbringing. Like many females of her generation, she had learned that women were not supposed to enjoy sex—or to know much about it. She had never indulged in sex talk of any kind. Sex had never been discussed when she was a child, and she never talked about it with the men she dated—or even with her husband when she'd been married. When her children had asked questions about sex, they were sent to their father, even though he knew little more than she did.

As a result, she was unable to communicate verbally about sex except very superficially. She could use the formal scientific names for body parts, but she had the usual antipathy for any informal or slangy sex language. Popular words that referred to any aspect of sex were, in her opinion, dirty. It didn't surprise me, then, that when I directed the conversation to her problems, she became almost tongue-tied. She could tell me about them in only the most general terms. Specifics meant using language she found repulsive. She could not discuss her own sexuality—her own reactions and emotions during sexual arousal—in a coherent manner.

But we did continue to talk. We explored various aspects of human emotion and love. We discussed the love of God and country, the love of a mother for her children, and sexual love—and through these safe, verbal channels we approached the reason for our being together, which was to discover why her sex life was so unsatisfactory. I continued my attempts to break through her language inhibitions so that we could more effectively pinpoint the reasons for her sexual unhappiness.

As our meetings continued, so did the talking. But we also learned to give and receive touching. I felt myself spellbound by her sensitive charm. Each time we met, she knew my feelings as soon as she saw me. She could sense my mood better than anyone I had ever met before. And she was interested in me without prying.

I tried my best to show her that same kind of loving concern, and I found no difficulty there at all. I could sense her moods, too, and I knew that our meetings were probably the greatest secret she had ever kept. For she couldn't tell her friends she was seeing me. They would never have understood.

Generally, a relationship like Emma's and mine continues for about fifteen weeks or so, under close supervision. Since this was my first experience, the supervision was very supportive—even though, at first, I was not that aware of it. I was too deeply involved in my work with Emma.

I remember the surprise I felt when I realized how fond of her I had grown. We weren't in love—I was sure of that—but many sessions were spent spontaneously doing things we both found we liked, sometimes without any need to verbalize our wishes.

I had not forgotten my reason for meeting with her. As Emma began to feel more comfortable with me, I encouraged her to express what she really felt, rather than just mouthing the conventional descriptions she had used at first. My goal was simple. I had to help her reach a point where she would willingly talk with me about subjects that she had never discussed before. I had a feeling of achievement each time she opened up a bit more.

What I had not expected was that she would have any effect on *me*. At first, I was too busy analyzing everything that happened between us to notice. This was the first time in my life that I was being totally objective about cultivating a friend. Then, gradually, I found myself becoming aware of the process and the mechanics involved. I learned to recognize the advantages of some of our exercises over the normal way a friendship starts.

From the first, we learned to negotiate. She'd say what she wanted and I'd reciprocate by telling her what I thought we really *should* be doing. Then we'd discuss the options and agree on a course of action. I didn't normally do that with friends, or even with my family.

We developed a rapport that allowed us both to learn. I came to know myself better, even though I had assumed that I already knew myself quite well. And she came to recognize at least one of the reasons for her problems. She became aware that she'd been so conditioned to think of sex as a "giving experience" that she'd been unable to receive sexual pleasure herself and had gradually begun using sex as a weapon in her relationships with men.

As she became increasingly conscious of her own sexuality, some strange things happened—personal, intimate things that never would have been brought to light in a conventional therapist's office.

Once, when we were doing an exercise that the therapist had suggested, it got out of hand. We were supposed to engage in what is called "nondemand genital pleasuring."

This kind of caressing is described as *sensate-focused* and is directed at teaching a client to accept pleasure. Client and surrogate alternate in touching each other, each taking personal satisfaction from the stroking. That is, the one doing the caressing focuses on the pleasure received from touching another person's body, while the passive partner focuses on receiving pleasure from being caressed. We were each to take enjoyment from what we did without being concerned with the other's reactions.

There should be no verbal communication during this activity unless there's discomfort. Then the receiver may say something like, "What you're doing feels wonderful. Could you move up a bit more?" Such a request puts no demand on the giver to continue caressing any one particular place, just as the giver, by taking enjoyment from doing the touching, demands nothing of the receiver. If the passive partner were instead to say, "That feels wonderful; keep on touching me there," a demand would be made to give special consideration to what felt best for the receiver, and the dynamics of the situation would change.

Emma and I started properly. I was first to caress her, enjoying for myself the feel of her body. For her, the emphasis was to be on *her* satisfaction. She understood that the intent of the exercise was to help her learn how to "take" pleasure—to go with her own feelings, at her own pace, without worrying about how her actions affected me. If either of us became aroused, we were to enjoy the sensations, but not make demands on the other person to do something about it.

Then we were to reverse positions. She was to continue taking pleasure, but this time in caressing me. No matter what my response (or lack of it), she was to concentrate on her own enjoyment of the exercise. She was to feel my body—my groin, my thighs, my belly, my testicles, my penis—thinking all the while of her own reactions, not mine. Orgasms and ejaculation were not the goal. I didn't want her to feel any pressure to "take care of" my erection if I became aroused.

As she was caressing me, she exclaimed that this was a unique and wonderful experience for her. Always, in the past, when she had touched a man's penis, it was to arouse him so he could have intercourse with her. What's more, she hadn't done it more than a few times, and then only reluctantly.

I was beginning to feel the pressure grow. "Stop," I said. "I'm about to come."

She made no attempt to comply. Instead she smiled and, with a look of glee, speeded up her hand movement until I could contain myself no longer. I exploded all over us both.

Talk about ambivalence! I was somewhat upset because she hadn't followed my instructions, and because I knew that the therapist wouldn't be pleased when we discussed this session later. At the same time, I felt so good I was speechless. For a while.

"Why didn't you stop when I asked you to?"

"I didn't want to." She seemed very smug. "I've never seen a man ejaculate before. Besides, I've never felt so powerful."

A logical pair of reasons. We dressed and headed for the therapist's office. And then I sensed that Emma, walking just a bit ahead of me, was very upset. In spite of what she had told me in the bedroom just moments before (the kind of message any partner would have believed), she was actually *angry* with me. But why?

Her fury burst forth as we settled down in the therapist's office. What right had I to come in her hand? Why didn't I have better control? Hadn't I told her the exercise was to be for *her* pleasure? Instead, I had *used* her hand—just like every man. She had *always* been used.

One thing was sure—she would never again let a man get that kind of power over her! Even if she wanted an orgasm, she wouldn't let a man have the satisfaction of giving her one.

The therapist was delighted with all that came from that one session. She now knew the messages Emma gave in the bedroom, and she could compare them with the entirely different feelings that Emma expressed during "talk therapy." Subsequently, we began to work with Emma to convince her that no matter how much of a stud a man is, he can't "give" a woman an orgasm unless she chooses to have one. And, if that is true, then *she* has the power—it is never his.

Our work together was not just sexual. Near the end of our relationship, when Emma was beginning to feel better about herself and closer to me than either of us cared to admit, she wondered aloud how we would relate in a nonsexual situation. With the therapist's approval, we then had a real date. We went to dinner, we danced, we drank wine—and we felt like two lovers out for a wonderful evening. As it drew to a close, I wasn't surprised that she felt comfortable enough to suggest we go to a motel.

I knew better than to agree. I assured her there was nothing I'd like more. But we had made an agreement with the therapist. This was to be a nonsexual experience—no more. If we ended up in a motel, our relationship would change.

She accepted my decision with obvious disappointment. The evening ended with just a fond good-night kiss. But I was aware now of what I had tried to ignore before. I had fallen in love with my client—and she with me.

During the next few sessions, we tried to work through our feelings. We talked a great deal and, I felt, were beginning to clear up the unwanted emotional involvement.

And then it was over. One day I came to the therapist's office as usual, expecting to see Emma, anticipating the meeting with delight. But she wasn't there. Instead, the therapist handed me a letter. Emma had realized, on her way home from the previous session, that she'd accomplished the goals she'd set for herself in therapy. She felt complete for the first time in her life. Complete—and wonderfully self-reliant. She thanked the therapist, explaining that she had learned so much during the office sessions and during the more intimate times with me. Now she realized how much courage she had needed to come for help, and she was thankful that she hadn't been disappointed.

I could barely read the words. I felt gratified that she was pleased with her new self and that she had accomplished what she wanted. But, at the same time, I felt a tremendous loss. I was aware—terribly aware—of the vacuum left in my life because Emma was gone. I wanted to tell her how much she had meant to me. I wanted to thank her. And I wanted to cry because I would never see her again.

Fortunately, the therapist could see my hurt—and she reached out to help me. For two sessions we talked. She convinced me that Emma had left abruptly because she knew a slow parting would be even more painful. And because I had succeeded in teaching her that when it was time for her to go back to her "real" life, she should do it.

But it still hurt. First, because I had to admit that in spite of my training and what I had been sure was the protection of professionalism, I had fallen in love with Emma. And, second, because I hadn't realized right away what was happening. With the therapist's help, I wrote a note to Emma expressing my feelings and my gratitude. I told her how, after each session, I had felt a twinge of guilt because I got so much out of our being together—

not necessarily sexually, but emotionally. I told her how much I had enjoyed my time with her, and how much I would miss her.

A few days later, the therapist and I received an answer—addressed to us both. Emma wrote as gently as she spoke. She understood what had happened between her and me, and she accepted it. It was a closeness she had never felt before. But she knew I had my own life, my own family. Now she was ready to find a similar relationship for herself. She thanked us for giving her the skills she needed to find such a life.

Emma said she had been prepared for the end of our three-way supportive learning relationship from the very beginning. We had helped her there, too, setting the entire experience up as a unit—beginning, middle, and end. She thanked us for that kind of preparation. It had made it possible for her to walk away when she knew the time had come.

I was stunned. The therapist and I had prepared our client for the close of our relationship, but no one had prepared me. Right then I knew I had a problem. Hereafter, I wanted more than just a breezy "thanks" from a client. I needed a chance to rehash the entire experience between us—to remember our successes and our failures. I needed a quiet time when I could give her back to herself, changed for having been in my keeping. I needed a session in which we could confront all the changes that had taken place in us both, because of our relationship. And I suspected that, in many cases, my clients would have the same needs.

I never saw Emma again, but I will be forever grateful to her. She taught me how much courage it took to disassociate from the past and future and to live for the moment. She taught me to be positive—to say "I will," not "I'll try." She taught me how much I was capable of loving—how capable we all are of loving—and that no matter how much love we give, there is still more available to us. I know now that the more people we truly love, the more capable we are of loving.

She taught me more. With her I learned how to redirect sexual energy into other areas of my life—and yet to take no energy from my sexual life. And I learned the thrill of oneness with another human being. It was a spiritual experience I will never forget.

Before my time with Emma, I had thought I knew what it meant to be a sex surrogate. Now I *really* knew. My worst fears had been realized—and proven to be harmless. I knew now that I could love any client I had without being afraid I would violate my agreement with her. I knew that I *had* to love a client if I was to show her how beautiful she was—and to be of help to her.

I'll never forget Emma, nor will I ever forget that she is responsible for many of my present strengths as well as for my continuing vulnerability. It was she who taught me that I could dare to be vulnerable.

What gives me pleasure is the knowledge that I taught her the very same thing.

2

YOU'RE A WHAT?
Every Man's Dream

O ver twenty years ago, while reading Masters and Johnson's report on their research, I became aware of the use they'd made of surrogates in sex therapy. I was, at the time, a practicing hypnotherapist, and I recalled how often I'd encountered female clients who were crying out for closeness and caring—women who wanted to be cuddled and held, not sexually, but in a supportive, protective manner. The idea of using a surrogate in their therapy intrigued me.

Many women who came to me had tried to express their need for closeness to their husbands or lovers and had failed. They had given signals that to them meant "I want to be cuddled, held, comforted," but their partners had interpreted those clues as meaning only one thing: "I want to get laid."

How nice it would be, I thought, to have a surrogate working with me who could establish a very close, intimate relationship with a client and learn how she really behaves when there's no demand for sex. Would she, then, as a result of that experience, open up and really talk to me? I knew that if she did, I could help her more than I could now with just my hypnotherapy. I had a client at the time who needed just what Masters and Johnson said a sex surrogate could provide. But was there a male surrogate in the Los Angeles area who could help me? I searched diligently with no success. Desperate, I even considered assuming the role myself.

The thought was intriguing. My imagination began running wild. I envisioned setting up a clinic in my home. I'd invite nothing but beautiful women (by my standards, of course) to my clinic and have them lining up at my door. And, boy, would I help them! I'd solve all their problems.

And, incidentally, maybe I'd solve some of my own.

There were no limits to the possibilities. I knew I had many buddies who'd love to go into the business with me. We could open up a nationwide chain. We'd franchise the idea and make millions. We'd . . . Fantasy soared.

I put the dream behind me. I recognized that no client is helped if the client–therapist relationship becomes anything except one for the *sole* benefit of the client. But later, even after the lady who had sparked the search for a surrogate in the first place had solved her problems, the thought remained. Could I be a sex surrogate?

The prospect teased my masculine ego. It was exciting—different. But it was impossible. I didn't have the training or the time. So I returned all my attention to my work and my role as husband and father. The dream died.

Ten years later, however, it came back to life like the phoenix.

My wife and I were having problems. After close to twenty years of marriage, we were growing apart. Our children were adults—or close to it. And we had changed, but not for the best, I felt. My wife had been so free-spirited and self-assured when we first met. Although alone in the world, she could cope with anything. Even after we married and the children came, she was always in control. But now, some years later, we both had become too dependent on each other. Though I had no problem with my reliance on her, I was fretting under the weight of her need for me. My impatience was showing. Everything I did to push her back onto her own feet seemed to backfire.

I felt I had to get away from the constant pressure, to relate to other people more, to find new zest and new interests in life. I was convinced that if I could have other sexual experiences, I could restore my feeling of self-importance. But I didn't want to break up with my wife. I just wanted her to release her hold on me enough to give me more freedom. Whatever I did had to be acceptable within the framework of our marriage.

So, once more the fantasy of becoming a sex surrogate commanded my attention. But almost as soon as it was reborn, overwhelming doubts returned. How could I even consider becoming a surrogate? What woman would permit it? What woman would step aside and allow her husband such freedom?

I could imagine my wife's reaction. She was accepting of my work with hypnotism, even though most of my clients were women. But could she as easily endure my actually having sex with someone else? I knew, of course, that there wouldn't be love in those relationships—only respect and trust. But could any wife accept and understand that? I doubted it, so the dream went back into hibernation, and I was at the point of dismissing the idea altogether.

My dissatisfaction with my life, however, was beginning to affect my work. I began to see fewer clients and, after a time, finally quit hypnotherapy entirely. I took a job as a computer engineer and began to settle into a dull routine.

And then, many years after that first germ of an idea stirred my interest, I felt the tug again. I was watching a TV talk show when Barbara Roberts, a sex therapist, spoke of her use of sex surrogates in dealing with certain problems brought to her by clients. She described the work being done under the auspices of therapists and in advanced centers for sexual studies. And she described her own Center for Social and Sensory Learning. I watched, fascinated. I knew then that I had to meet her.

My dream had been brought back to life again. I *had* to be a sex surrogate. Never mind that so far as I knew there was no such thing as a male surrogate. Never mind that I was probably sharing a fantasy every red-blooded man must have at least once in his life. Like many men who've reached middle age, I wasn't sure what I wanted out of life. My goals were unclear—more so than they'd been when I was younger—and my needs seemed to be changing.

I went to the Center for Social and Sensory Learning in the San Fernando Valley and met Barbara Roberts. That meeting changed my life. But I didn't immediately qualify as a surrogate. Not a chance. First, I was to come to a Sexual Enrichment Experience class that was taught at the Center. It was, she explained, an experiential class for people who wanted to get in touch with themselves—who wanted to learn about their own sensuality. After signing up for the class, I went away shaking my head in disbelief. I was sure I'd gone out of my mind. What sort of nonsense was this, anyway? What did they mean by "get in touch with oneself"? But I had to take that class to convince them I was serious about wanting to be a surrogate. I had to be "evaluated" first.

"Evaluated!" The whole idea amused me. I was convinced that the qualities they were looking for were insubstantial, illusory concepts created in the active minds of people who'd actually make their decision based on far more substantial considerations—like how many classes I'd be willing to pay for. Or, maybe, just on how long I could go without having an orgasm. Don't ask why I persisted. I felt as if I were swimming in a mirage. But I was too stubborn to quit, I suppose. I spent some fifty-odd hours in classes at the Center with eleven other strangers, all of whom seemed as lost as I was. But, little by little, I absorbed the wealth of knowledge being offered.

From my studies in college, I was already acquainted with all the anatomical differences between men and women. But I now learned about the importance of a well-conditioned pubococcygeus (p.c.) muscle, in both men and women, if the greatest amount of sexual pleasure is to be achieved.

I learned that both male and female surrogates receive exactly the same kind of training. Both use the same tools—empathy, caring, patience, some expertise in anatomy, an understanding of meditation, and the ability to exert physical and mental control over bodily functions. Both develop the same abilities to communicate, to listen to—and to hear—what is said. These tools, which work so well in the treatment of men plagued by impotence, premature ejaculation, or a flagging libido, also serve in treating women who are pre-orgasmic, have pain during intercourse, or lack sexual interest.

I also learned about myself and my masculinity—about the difference between being macho and being male. I became conscious of my feminine side and its characteristics and what it means to be a woman. And I learned the difference between sexuality and sensuality. I truly experienced what I'd known only intellectually before—that the brain, not the genitals, is the center of sexual sensations.

This newly acquired knowledge fascinated me.

After the course was over and I'd said good-bye to the friends I'd made there, I went on with my studies, attending lectures and workshops that expanded my understanding even further. But I began to grow impatient. I was a good student. I knew now what was needed for this new career. When would I get to try out my skills?

However, even though impatient and convinced of my qualifications, I wasn't yet ready to set up a practice of my own—to fulfill the fantasy that had started so long ago. There was more to learn. My training was not complete until I had spent fifteen sessions as an intern surrogate under the close supervision of a sex therapist.

Is being a surrogate worth all that study? A thousand times yes!

Is being a surrogate at all what I expected it to be, back when I was spinning all those wild dreams? Not at all!

I now had learned to recognize women as people and was able to put aside considerations as to whether they were conventional, old-fashioned, or liberated until later, and then only if those characteristics affected our relationship. This new insight taught me to enjoy women, and men as well, more than I ever had before—because I could now appreciate them for what they were without making demands that they be something else just to suit me. For the first time in my life I listened intently when people spoke. And, marvelously, the increased awareness triggered memories I had thought were buried—memories that helped me empathize with the women I hoped someday to help.

I once knew a man who took a delightful lady out for a wonderful evening. They went to dinner at a beautiful restaurant by the sea. The wine was outstanding, the dinner superb. They danced and laughed together. They stood on the sand and let the wind ruffle their hair. Everything was perfect.

It was late when he brought her home. She thanked him, kissed him good night, and vanished behind her door.

He was furious! A week later, he was still angry when he told me about it. "I spent all that time and money and didn't get laid!"

I hadn't felt much sympathy for him. I told him he'd given no thought to the time they'd spent together. Even while he was experiencing the pleasant dinner, the smooth dancing, the walk on the beach, he was thinking of getting her into bed. He hadn't bothered to notice that he was having fun.

He pondered awhile before ruefully admitting that he'd probably have acted the same way even if he had been successful in getting her to bed. He'd have been so concentrated on reaching his own orgasm that he wouldn't have enjoyed the long evening buildup at all.

I'd been a little like him in my youth. But I knew now that I'd never be in danger of slipping back into that impatient attitude. After my hours of training, I'd learned to savor every moment of pleasure.

I was actually surprised that I had anything to learn in that area. I'd never been one to rush through a sexual encounter to orgasm. I enjoyed the touching too much. I'd often wondered, in the past, at the practice of so many men who take the most enjoyable human encounter we can have and hurry through it. Why not savor it to the utmost? Why not extend it, experiencing the greatest pleasure possible?

It should be obvious to most people that many sexual dysfunctions are due to pressure, to anxiety, to the demand to perform, and to the desire to hurry things along so as to "get to the good part." At the Center, we learned that "the good part" begins with the first touch and continues as long as we let it. With such an attitude we don't fall victim to the drive toward sexual success. We know that the harder we strive for it, the more elusive it becomes.

And we got our priorities straight. We asked the same old questions but we found new answers. What is success in sex? A certain number of orgasms? Being able to keep an erection for X number of minutes?

Not at all! Success in a sexual encounter comes from moment-by-moment enjoyment. Many women seem to know this without any training. The problem is, they don't know how to guide a partner into sharing this pleasure. But the lesson can be taught. Surrogates understand that. It's the understanding that allows them to help others.

So what is a sex surrogate? It's a person who's gone through the required hours of training and internship and who works with a licensed sex therapist—a marriage and family counselor, a social worker specializing in sex therapy, a psychologist, a psychiatrist, or even a minister or priest who has special training. It's the therapist who is in charge. It's the therapist who selects the surrogate who will be most compatible with his or her client.

Whenever possible, a therapist encourages a prospective client to bring along his or her "significant other." That means wife or husband—or lover. When that happens, a surrogate isn't needed.

But there are times when a client either has no significant other or the problem to be treated is intimately involved with that relationship. If the latter is true, the wife or husband or lover is just the wrong person to try to help. Emotional involvement that's too intense can get in the way of therapy.

It's a bit like teaching your wife or sister or brother to drive a car. You may be an excellent driver yourself, but you may be an unskilled or impatient teacher. You get upset when something goes wrong. That's why so many people who have lots of friends and relatives who know how to operate a car still go to a driving school to learn.

In the same sense, we sex surrogates are simply professionals in a specific field. And we do everything we can to maintain our professional standing. For me, that meant affiliating myself with the International Professional Surrogates Association, or IPSA.

IPSA is based in California, and it has probably the most stringent code of ethics of any profession anywhere in the country. Its membership is small, and it requires that applicants prove they've received the proper training before they're accepted. In addition to being a support group for working surrogates, IPSA also provides a referral service for clients who are looking for sex therapists who use surrogates as well as for therapists who are looking for surrogates.

IPSA conducts its own training classes for prospective surrogates, and members are in the process of setting up a training team that will travel nationwide to teach prospective surrogates and instruct therapists who wish to learn how to utilize surrogates in their practice.

Members of IPSA range in age from the late twenties to the late fifties. There are probably seven or eight female surrogates to every male. We come from all walks of life, seldom making our livings solely as surrogates. We're housewives, teachers, nurses, lawyers, engineers, business people. Many of us have degrees in unrelated fields, but a large number of IPSA members have previous experience in the area of mental health. As surrogates, some specialize in working with disabled men or women, others in working with sex offenders. There are gay surrogates and bisexual surrogates. There are even male and female surrogates who will pair up to work with a couple in role-modeling.

In our modern society, we have a habit of classifying people by their jobs. An engineer is a certain type of man, a laboratory researcher another. An elementary-school teacher is judged to be outgoing, while a college professor is often expected to be absentminded. Maybe one thing that upsets many people is that sex surrogates can't be so easily classified. How do you categorize a person who is a nurse by day and a sex surrogate in the evening? What is the proper classification of a teacher who's a sex surrogate on weekends?

What is it, precisely, surrogates do that can't be done by therapists? They establish an intimate relationship within a specific framework. I've never worked with a client yet where we haven't unearthed deeply hidden material because of our closeness—material that speeds up therapy and that would not have come to light had only conventional "talk therapy" been utilized. Usually, even the client had no idea that she harbored such hidden secrets.

"But sex surrogates are really whores!"

We still hear that accusation—sometimes even from would-be clients. It hurts when, after all the training that enables me to help a woman dig down to the hurt that hampers her sexual enjoyment, I still have to defend myself against that condemnation.

It hurts because it just isn't true. What prostitute has spent hours in classes learning psychology and special techniques (not necessarily physical) for drawing out confidences and creating an environment of trust and understanding? What prostitute works only under the supervision of a sex therapist and takes part in talk sessions following almost every meeting with a client?

What's more, our goals are different. A prostitute may

have a warm relationship with a specific person. But in the long run, she's only interested in an orgasm for her customer, quickly and with the least exertion on her part. And money. Maybe that's her main goal—more money.

As surrogates, we have entirely different goals when we work with clients. Our aim is to improve the quality of life for each person by helping him or her develop an improved self-image and gain increased self-confidence. Sex contact is one aspect of that picture—but it's far from being the only important thing that takes place.

And therein lies the main difference. When a prostitute is through with her customer, he's experienced momentary sexual release. She's gained some money. But life hasn't changed for either of them.

However, when a sex surrogate and his or her client separate, the client goes away feeling better about life, more self-confident and serene. If the surrogate has been successful and the sex therapy has been effective, the client returns to the "real world" with a new vision of his or her place in it. Generally, such a client will never need a sex surrogate—or sex therapy—again.

The surrogate, too, has grown because of the encounter. He or she has dared to expose private vulnerabilities so that the client will gain courage. He or she has shared in the growth of another's inner strength and new understanding of life. Is it any wonder that, unlike prostitutes, sex surrogates feel good about themselves and are proud of what they do? And is it any wonder that they refuse to quit, even when their work is misunderstood?

3

PUTTING MY HOUSE
IN ORDER
There's More to Love Than Sex

Those first months at the Center for Social and Sensory Learning were bittersweet. In class I was learning more about myself each day, but my situation at home was growing more difficult. My wife seemed to think that the attempts I made to get her to behave autonomously only proved that I no longer loved her. But I did love her, and I wanted her—of all women—to be happy, both emotionally and sexually.

As I advanced in my classes at the Center, however, she began to resent my "practicing" on her. Try as I might, I couldn't convince her that any small changes I made in touching her body were done out of love. She was sure I was just doing "homework." It took me a while to realize that, in a way, she was right.

As we continued to grow further apart, she assumed that I had taken a lover, and I must admit the possibility crossed my mind that she had, too. The thought hurt. To compensate for her rejection, I began to devote even more time to my studies, and to hobbies in which she couldn't participate. I was frightened and lonely—feeling isolated from both her and the children.

We were taking less and less. I think we both feared what might be said. I know I did. But I still loved her. Even dependent as she now appeared, I loved her as much as I had that day when I saw her at an open-house party—the beautiful girl in the flowered dress.

Way back then, I'd known I never wanted to be apart from her. Me, the run-around, macho man who had taken years to learn that women wanted gentle men, not braggarts. I was hooked that night—and I never again wanted to be free.

The realization overwhelmed me. Something was wrong with my marriage. I couldn't deny that. But something was right, too. If we'd wanted to separate—if divorce had been the answer—one of us would have said so. We'd have moved from this uncomfortable spot we seemed to be stuck in.

I came to this bright conclusion in the middle of a class at the Center, and I could hardly wait to get home. I wanted to share with my wife this new recognition of our love. I wanted her to know how much I needed to be near her and to touch her. But everything seemed to delay me. I know now that was good. If I'd rushed home, I'd have started with a flood of words.

By the time I did reach home that night, I knew talking wouldn't work. Not at this point. Words were fine for making plans, discussing finances—even for explaining small changes in our physical relationship—but they wouldn't serve to eliminate the estrangement that troubled us now. We'd had enough words. They were too easy to misunderstand. I had to show by my actions that I enjoyed being with her—touching her, loving her. I realized that I wanted to caress her, not to arouse her for sex, but just because touching her gave me pleasure. And I had to let her know that I understood at last that sex alone couldn't bridge the gap that had developed between us.

I had tried to practice the exercises I was learning in class when I was with her, but they hadn't worked. Now I knew why. Always, I had focused on her reactions to my touch, as if I were performing some magic by caressing her. Now I knew what was missing. I needed to show her that the real reason for my wanting to touch and caress her was that it gave *me* pleasure. Only then would she begin to trust me again when I said I loved her.

She was waiting up. I kissed her, holding her in my arms. "I want to give you a massage."

I felt her body stiffen, but I was not going to allow her to refuse. Taking her hand, I led her into the bedroom. We undressed in silence, but I was sure I knew what was going through her mind. She expected me to want sex. I always had in the past when I got her into bed with me. I was certain that she believed my reference to a massage was just a new ploy, needed now because of our odd estrangement.

After I laid my trousers aside, I pulled out a small bottle of oil like the kind we used at the Center. "Turn over on your stomach." I spoke while I was still across the room, repressing an urge to smile at her surprised glance.

When she lay on her stomach, I approached the bed. I poured the oil slowly, just the right amount to make my hands move easily over her body. As I touched her, I could feel the tension. I knew she thought that at any minute I would stop and expect her to "do something" about my erection. Because I did have one. Her body, even after years of marriage and two children, was still beautiful.

I had now practiced enough at school so that I showed no hesitation in my caressing. I stroked her in the nondemand, sensate-focused way I had been taught. As my fingers moved smoothly over her hips, I felt her begin to relax. When I turned her over and still didn't concentrate on her genitals, the relaxation increased. My erection was gone, but I didn't miss it. I was too involved in showing my love.

And she recognized the difference in my feelings. This was the first time in all our years together that we were naked together in bed, touching, holding, loving, and I hadn't made one single overture that might lead to intercourse. I had only one wish—to show her my love. I realized that I didn't even want intercourse. Right then it would only have gotten in the way.

I realized something else, too. When I had first started surrogate training, she had fluctuated between an avid interest in every detail of each session and complete disregard for what was going on in my life. I knew, suddenly, that she'd been afraid to hear the truth, "knowing" that her worst suspicions, that I was touching and loving someone else, would be confirmed. If we'd talked about it, that's all she would have heard, no matter what I might have said.

But by touching her this way, I could show her a more meaningful picture of what I'd been learning. I could demonstrate my love in a manner I'd never been capable of before. The realization of how important this new communication was only increased my desire to express my love for her in this tactile manner.

It was late before I sensed that her need was gone. Her body was more relaxed than it had ever been, even after a wildly amorous session. I dropped beside her on the bed and took her in my arms.

But she had other plans. Now she took the oil and returned the caresses that had told her of my love. Like me, she avoided the genitals. They weren't the object of our embrace. Instinctively, she used the same sensate-focus way of touching that I had learned in my class. Feeling her fingers lovingly caress my body, I knew she understood what I had wanted to tell her.

Only when she had finished did we talk. The barriers were gone—at last. I told her of my fear that she had a lover and wanted a divorce. She told me she'd been sure that my putting money into "her" account had been an overture to my leaving to be with someone else.

We talked about our clinging need for each other and our pushing each other away. We faced the futility of jealousy and our continued need for mutual support. And we shared the understanding that if either of us had truly wanted a divorce, or had wanted to run off with someone else, we'd have done so long ago.

She told me how much she'd wanted me to be close to her without being sexual. Not that she didn't want sex. She delighted in the sex we shared. But this need for intimacy was so critical. It made her feel safe, appreciated, and desired. And it made her respect herself more because she knew, in this deeply personal way, that I loved her.

For the first time since I began classes at the Center, I dared to explain that this was what I was learning to give my clients. As a surrogate, I could help women reach this state of self-acceptance that meant so much. But there would be a difference—there would always be a difference—between what I shared with my clients and what she and I had between us.

With her, I could be myself. I could show my needs and have them filled. With my clients, I would always be concerned only with them. When their needs were satisfied, the relationship would be over. My "home base" would be with my wife—always.

It seems almost a miracle, the effect of that night of communion. Since then, she has taken the same attitude toward my surrogate clients that she had toward my hypnotherapy clients, or any relationship I might have with another woman. She trusts me to keep centered on her. She knows that while I'm helping my clients, I'm getting a certain amount of satisfaction in return. But this is apart from, and yet strangely because of, my close relationship with her. Never, no matter how involved I get with a client, do I have even the slightest wish to change what has now become the most wonderful part of my life—the unity I feel with my wife.

After that special night, we both were finally able to appreciate the value of my surrogate training. Here we were, two loving people who had lived together for years, yet our relationship had benefited from the body massage that is only one small part of the surrogate program. She knew, also, that very few people realize such intimacy is possible—or know how to achieve it if they do. I suspect she visualized my duties as those of a new kind of saint, pointing the way to emotional freedom and happiness. And I know now that, in a way, I had the same image.

My first case exploded that fantasy. I realized after my encounter with Emma, my first "real life" client, that I was no saint. I was a very human man who had learned a lot in the year just ended, but who was still an easy victim of all the foibles I'd possessed before the training. I still enjoyed sex. I still got horny—sometimes when I shouldn't. But over that old me I had now superimposed a new identity with new knowledge and skills. I knew how to control my sex drive. I was thoroughly aware of my own responsibility for my erections and orgasms. And this knowledge allowed me to control those sometimes inappropriate behavior patterns that appear to be "natural" to all men.

Every man I've ever met has grown up liking *sex*. I learned I had one small advantage over most of them: I liked *women*, too. I had never quite recognized this difference until I began studying at the Center. I really liked women for themselves. And I admired the courage they all showed as they tried to survive in our very male-oriented society. Because I liked and admired women, I respected them—not as angels, but as vibrant, living human beings.

My experience with my wife had shown me the value of intimacy in a marriage. My first surrogate work with Emma taught me the manner in which intimacy can work in a temporary relationship. And it taught me one other thing—that I would learn as much from each of my clients as they learned from me. A person who isn't constantly learning is stagnating, both mentally and emotionally. I knew now that only by my own growth and continuing vitality, both mental and physical, could I help my clients to accept life and their own sexuality, which is such an integral part of it.

I know I have the total support of both my children. What I have learned has helped them in their relationships, and they are both able to pass on valuable information to their friends. My daughter has asked me to speak before groups to which she belongs. She's majoring in psychology, wants to work in sex therapy, and has suggested that she might use me as a surrogate for *her* clients when she starts her practice.

There are some friends who will be surprised when they read this book. They know I'm in "sex therapy," but they don't know exactly what it is I do. Some may not approve. But that's their problem, not mine.

When I began to write this book, I discussed the entire matter with my wife and children. Should I use a pseudonym? All three agreed that I shouldn't. They felt it was important for me to show that I was proud of what I did, and that I had their full support. Using a false name would have made a joke of my claim to be proud of my profession. And I know they were right.

I now find myself to be one of the few male sex surrogates in the country, and one of a small fraction of those who are in a position to be openly recognized. But the question might be asked, why do I choose this form of disclosure? I don't do it because I want or expect admiration. On the contrary, I recognize that many people will still have a difficult time understanding how my wife can put up with the intimacy I share with my clients. Yet that is the very reason why I know I must speak up.

I feel the need to talk about my work because I know many couples suffer in silence, longing to communicate but unable to get beyond the barrier of words. I work with women who need to experience intimacy with someone—a husband or a lover—but who find that, when they reach out for love, all they get is sex.

But maybe that isn't the main reason. It's easy to say I'm doing this to help those women who look for caressing and touching and get only intercourse. But that isn't being completely honest. I'm speaking up because I know what true intimacy with my wife has done for my life—and for hers. (And I know that as macho as men behave, they need intimacy, too—often more than the women I deal with on a day-to-day basis.) Being a surrogate allows me to provide that intimacy for a few select women. But this book can open the door to a wonderful life-changing experience for anyone who chooses to read it—and to think about what I have to say.

4

THE SINGLE CLIENT
A Matter of Trust

Most sex therapists prefer to treat couples. By this I mean they prefer that any single person coming to them for therapy bring a partner. But this isn't always easy. Many single men and women seeking sex therapy do so because they can't relate to their lovers in a satisfactory manner. They may have floated from one relationship to another without ever achieving satisfaction. Sometimes the problem is sexual. But not many people actually have damaged or malfunctioning sex organs. Most often, the sexual difficulties they encounter are caused by past traumatic experiences and by the fear and anger such unpleasant events have generated.

Because of this, these singles are unable to establish close relationships with anyone. They live in lonely isolation, afraid of intimacy, yet lost and depressed because they can't experience it. What's more, when they seek help, they have no one who's willing to go into therapy with them.

No one, that is, except a surrogate.

So most of my clients are single women. They have an

assortment of problems. One may be totally unable to feel any sexual sensations. Another may be so fearful of men that she won't allow them to get near her. Yet another may be what men call a "ball buster," a woman who's insatiable, who can't seem to be satisfied by any man.

One woman came to therapy because she couldn't endure any form of sex other than oral contact. Another came to get help in understanding her fantasies. Many of them can't have orgasms. Occasionally, a client referred to a surrogate has such severe problems that it appears she can't accept any help at all.

If I'm successful, these clients leave me and the therapist with a newfound ability to relate to others. They change from loners into vital women who are capable of forming real attachments and establishing long-lasting relationships.

Many women who are in therapy to learn how to have orgasms also have problems relating to their ability to feel. This isn't surprising. We're taught from childhood to repress our "baser" sensations. Men can't repress sexual feelings as easily as women, since they have to touch their penises when they urinate. Women, however, can so totally ignore their genitals that they may actually lose the ability to recognize sensations stirred up when genital contact does take place. These two difficulties—not having orgasms and not really feeling sexual contact—are closely related to each other, as well as to other deep-seated problems that often keep their victims from living full lives.

One of these well-entrenched problems is a lack of trust. In an ideal society, we would learn as children to be trusting. Unfortunately for them as well as for society, many children are taught fear, rather than trust, as a basic attitude. I don't know if this is more common for women than for men. (Probably not.) But I do know that lack of trust can destroy any chance a person may have of establishing a love relationship, or of achieving success and happiness. If this condition is extreme, a person can live behind a protective shell of defenses so strong that no other human being can penetrate it. When this happens, therapy must first address the fear. Only after trust has been established can constructive advances be made in dealing with the related social and sexual problems.

One particular client illustrates this vital need we all have to trust not only others but, most important, ourselves as well. I was called by a female therapist and asked if I would be interested in working with a very special woman. This client, Angie, was twenty-three years old and had been under treatment for some time. She had developed anorexia nervosa, a pathological loss of appetite, when she was eighteen and had spent several weeks in a mental hospital against her will. She had never had a good relationship with her parents, who blamed her for their personal difficulties, although they, themselves, had many psychological problems and a marriage that had been in trouble long before Angie was born.

Angie was an extreme case. On a scale of one to ten, she had zero sexual knowledge and skills. She was, not surprisingly, a virgin. In her cure, a vital aspect of surrogate therapy is highlighted—our close contact permitted her to begin to trust me. And as that trust grew, her chances of recovery increased.

Angie had been to several other therapists, all of whom had given up because of communication difficulties. Her skills in that area, if not zero, were certainly on the low end of the scale. She often misunderstood what was said to her. One therapist had told her that she *could* have sex with men if she chose to. She interpreted that to mean she *should* have sex, and she would have complied had she known what to do. She had tried dating but had been terrified when she found herself alone with a man. She was afraid he might hurt her, yet she was totally unaware of what it was he might try to do. She didn't even know how to kiss. When she asked her therapist to show her, she didn't dare allow any contact, so she held up her hand to be used as a model.

Angie suffered from vaginismus, a condition in which the vaginal muscles are in an almost constant state of spasm. Hers was so severe that her gynecologist couldn't insert a speculum to give her a pelvic exam. Even when he tried to insert his little finger, it caused her so much pain that she was considering never going to him again. And she had never consciously seen a penis or a vagina. When the gynecologist asked her if she wanted a mirror to see herself, a common practice today, she shrieked "No!" and went into mild hysterics.

Though she had a normal I.Q., Angie was very naive. Again, on a one-to-ten scale, her social skills would have rated about a two. She had been told many myths that filled her with fear. One was particularly destructive. She had been informed that if she touched herself "down there," something big and hard would grow in her. I assume the reference was to the clitoris, but it might have been to pregnancy. She pictured this big hard thing to be about the size of a baseball bat, so she carefully avoided ever touching herself in the danger area because of her certainty that such a growth would be painful.

On her last "date," she had been out with a young man who had tried to fondle her. She had been so frightened that he had backed off. But then, maybe in an attempt to get her interest, he had taken out his penis and started to masturbate. She didn't know what he was doing or what that "thing" was. But the sound of his groans and the sight of what appeared to be a big hard growth "down there" on his body terrified her. She ran out of the car and walked home, convinced that if she'd stayed with him, he'd have killed her.

On our first meeting, I saw a rather pretty girl, slightly overweight and extremely shy. She blushed when I walked into the room. She was exceptionally docile, totally lacking in assertiveness. The therapist was also in the room, and Angie would not look at either of us, even when she spoke. I could sense her fear of me, but I also knew she wouldn't have the courage to walk out, or even to refuse to let me work with her.

Because she was obviously afraid to go to another room with me, we stayed in the therapist's office for our entire first encounter, contrary to normal procedure. Angie sat on a chair and I sat on a large sofa, facing her. I had already assured her that I'd never pressure her to do anything she didn't want to, but I could see she barely understood what I meant. Now I had to illustrate my promise and plant the seeds of mutual trust.

The therapist left the room. I sat across from Angie, aware that she would not initiate any conversation, so, as a start to our becoming acquainted, I asked her about anything I felt might be of interest to a young woman her age. She responded to every question with quiet obedience. I asked, she answered. Nothing seemed to arouse any enthusiasm or excitement. The session was drawing to an end, and I knew I had made no progress. There was only one possible step we could take. Before we parted this first time, I wanted her to let me do a sensate-focused hand caress.

"Angie, would you mind coming over here and sitting next to me?"

She didn't answer. Instead, she fairly leaped up and landed beside me, like a frightened child who's just been told she's done something wrong. She hadn't even considered whether she was willing to do as I asked. Her response was automatic—her usual reaction. She was conditioned to regard every request or suggestion as a command, which she then obeyed without hesitation.

I put a small pillow on her lap. "I want to caress your hand. This pillow will help you feel safe."

I began to stroke her hand gently, aware of her tenseness. She clearly expected me to touch her somewhere else as well. But when I remained true to my word, she did relax a little, though I could still feel tightness in the muscles of her fingers.

When I decided I'd done all I could for the first time, I asked her to do my hand. She complied immediately, performing a carbon copy of my caress, but without any apparent pleasure. She was doing what she'd been asked to do—nothing more. She did seem a bit more comfortable, although she still sat stiffly upright. At one point, I thought I detected the hint of a smile. When the therapist returned and asked how things were going, Angie looked up. "Fine. This is fun."

"Then you'd like to work with Jerry?"

"Yes. I think he'll be all right."

"Even if you're alone for more than ten minutes?"

"Yes." She didn't sound confident, but at least the words were the right ones. I knew I had to prove them to be true.

Together, we reviewed what would happen. Each time Angie came for therapy, she would also have a session with me. Both she and I would take direction from the therapist, reporting to her weekly to discuss what happened when Angie and I were alone together.

The second session brought out more of her background. In a way, she had lived a "Cinderella" life. She had never been physically abused, but neither had she been treated with kindness. She wasn't allowed, for example, to use the hot water until everyone else in the family had bathed. This meant she couldn't bathe until late at night or early in the morning. As soon as she was past childhood, she was expected to pay her own expenses, even though she had almost no job skills. And, because she had no idea why she was dealt with so badly, she worried continually that what little she earned would be taken away from her.

I was feeling very sympathetic toward her at this point, but I knew I had to do more than just listen and give her understanding. "It's time we got to work. I'd like us to have a special way of greeting. How about a hug as our private way of saying hello?"

She blushed, stood up, and let me hug her. Her body was stiff, and she did not return my embrace.

I dropped my arms and stood facing her. "When two people hug, both of them put their arms up, like I did. And they both enjoy the feeling of closeness. Let's try again. Remember, I won't touch you anywhere except on your back near your shoulders. I promise."

This time she held me, too, and I sensed a little less tension than before. I decided that was all I could expect so early in our relationship. Maybe I could risk going on with the exercises that normally were part of the first meeting. If she was too frightened, I would back off.

I spoke quietly. "Now I'm going to feel your face. Just your face. I want you to relax and enjoy my touch."

She didn't, of course. I could feel the tension in every muscle. When I finished, she stood quietly, waiting for my next "command."

Pushing back my despair, I continued. "Now I want you to touch my face. Do it just for yourself. I want you to feel what it's like to touch me, and I don't want you to worry about how I react." I saw the look of fear and hurried on. "Don't be afraid. I might smile or twitch my nose if you tickle me. But I won't touch you at all. I'll keep my arms at my sides. I promise."

She seemed reassured. Her first contact with my face was tenuous. I barely felt her fingers against my skin. But the pressure increased gradually. After a few minutes, she stopped. "Wow, this is nice! I've never touched anyone before." She actually sounded interested.

I smiled, but I didn't answer her. With a fleeting smile in return, she went back to fingering my beard and mustache. When she was through, I was sure she had relaxed a little more. She stood before me without any visible sign of fright, and she even looked up at my face, though not into my eyes.

We still had some time, and I didn't dare go faster with the steps toward intimacy, so I stepped over to the desk and pulled a hairbrush out of my kit. "May I brush your hair?"

She blushed, obviously embarrassed. But she didn't refuse. She was still reacting to what she considered commands. Obediently, she sat in the chair I indicated. Once more her body was stiff. I could feel the tension as I began to pull the brush through her hair, and I realized how little impact our first exercises had had on her basic fear. Yet, as I brushed, I again felt the same small easing of tightness that had encouraged me earlier.

When I finished, she stood up, took the brush without being asked, and waited until I took her place. Then, silently, she began to brush my hair. Once more, her initial acts were carbon copies of my own.

However, very soon the differences between us caused her to giggle softly. I have a bald spot that could not be brushed. I had to resist the urge to cheer, for I knew this reaction of hers was significant. She wasn't responding to a command or question. For the first time, she was behaving spontaneously, even though her reactions were still very reserved.

She finished her chore after taking just about as much time with my shorter hair as I had with her long tresses. I stood up and we said good-bye. I looked down at her, expecting the same evasiveness I had encountered when we were first introduced, but instead my eyes met hers. And, most surprising, she was not blushing.

I spoke quietly. "I have to go now. Will I see you next week?"

She nodded and took a step toward me. All on her own, she reached up and hugged me gently. It was a hurried embrace, as if she still wasn't sure such an act was permissible. But she had actually reached out on her own!

I felt like crying. Was this, I wondered, the first time this fragile girl had dared to communicate nonverbally with another human being? I hugged her back, gently, hoping she would feel my tenderness and know that I cared very much for her and understood how brave she was.

She was smiling when she returned the following week. She embraced me without being told, but her body was still tense.

My first question as we sat facing each other was simply a polite inquiry. "How are you today?"

"I'm afraid of everything," she answered.

Surprised at her candor, I asked more specific questions. She seemed ready to talk about her fears and doubts, but she still needed prodding before she spoke. I had to ask direct questions or she lapsed into silence.

At last I asked the obvious. "Why don't you ever volunteer an idea? All you do is answer me."

"I don't know what to say."

I thought for a moment. "One way to get over that

kind of nervousness is just by asking questions. I do it. When I first meet a client, I ask a lot of questions. I learn from the answers, and it helps us get acquainted." I paused for a moment and then continued. "Why don't you try it? Ask anything you want to know. I'll try to answer."

At first her questions were very formal. She was doing what I'd told her to do—no more. But soon they became more spontaneous. She actually wanted to hear the answers.

"I wish I knew how to act with a boy. I'd love to date. But I'm so afraid I'll be grabbed. And I don't even know how to kiss."

"Let's play a game. We'll pretend we're on a date."

She hesitated for a moment. "What will I wear?"

"I can't answer that. Why don't you go to a dress shop and look around? You'll get an idea of what's stylish now. Talk to a clerk there. I'm sure she'll help you find out what looks good on you. You don't have to buy everything she suggests. If clothes in that store are too expensive, you can go someplace else to buy."

She nodded and we went on with our pretend date. We got into a car and tried out different ways of starting a conversation. We pretended to park in lover's lane and I had her sit close to me. I told her I'd act like a grabber trying to feel her up. Then I suggested ways she could fend off such advances and still make the boy feel comfortable with her refusal to let him take advantage of her.

I tried all sorts of approaches, suggesting different responses for each one. To my delight, she actually seemed to be enjoying what we were doing. I knew she felt safe, and I was pleased. When we'd finish one kind of approach, she'd suggest another. And then came the clincher. "What do I do if I want to let him go all the way?"

I took a deep breath. "That comes later. You're not ready yet."

"Oh." She didn't seem disappointed. "Will you at least show me how to kiss on the lips?"

I nodded. I showed her how to put her hands on my shoulders, and I gently touched lips with hers. Then, as with the different approaches, we tried different kinds of kisses. I used both hard pressure and soft. I shifted positions until we found a way that felt good to both of us. I thought that ended the lesson on kissing, but she was being more adventuresome than I realized.

"How do you French kiss?"

I showed her, moving very slowly. When I leaned back, she met my gaze. "Why would anyone want to do that?"

I talked then about sexual excitement, finally pretending to be aroused to show her how someone in that state might behave. She giggled when I began to breathe heavily. She had decided this was great fun after all. She volunteered that maybe the man who had scared her on her last date was really just aroused. I agreed. But I didn't try to relate his arousal to his enlarged penis, or even to get her to recognize that big hard thing as being a penis. She wasn't ready for that yet.

At the end of this session, she was once more fearful. "I have to go to the gynecologist again in two weeks for a Pap smear. It always hurts so much." She shook her head. "He told me to put my own fingers in there, to loosen it up. But I can't do that."

I wished that we were further along, so I could help her overcome her fear of touching herself, but there wasn't time. "You really should do as he suggests. There's nothing bad about touching yourself. And if you do, your visits will be easier."

She nodded, but I wasn't a bit sure she would act on my urging any more than she had on the advice of the gynecologist. I didn't want to nag, though. We hugged again and she was gone. I was pleased to report to the therapist the progress she'd made.

I had a talk with the therapist again before our next session, and we decided that Angie and I should try more touching, since we seemed to have broken down some of her barriers. Maybe we could even try a sensate-focused back caress, which would require that we strip to the waist. I agreed, knowing that Angie had made progress. But I wasn't prepared for the change that had taken place since our last meeting, only a week before.

Angie started the fourth session by giving me a warm hug. I could actually feel her hands against my back. And then, without my asking, she blurted out that she'd tried putting her fingers into her vagina and it hadn't hurt. I congratulated her, suggesting that she keep it up. And then, encouraged, I asked her how she felt about trying a sensate-focused caressing of the back.

"You don't have to do anything you don't want to. Remember that. But if you decide that we can do this, we'll have to take off our tops."

She grew very quiet. "That wouldn't be right. People shouldn't be in their underclothes together unless they're married. They shouldn't even touch anyplace except maybe the hands and face."

I hoped I didn't show my disappointment. "Okay. In that case . . ." I fished wildly in my mind for some alternate exercise that might build on what we had already accomplished.

"Hey, what the hell!" The brightness of her tone—and her words—startled me. "That's why I'm here, isn't it? If I'm ever going to learn, I guess I'll just have to jump in and do it!"

It was tempting to remark on how uncharacteristic such an outburst was, but I didn't. Instead, I began to unbutton my shirt. I tried not to show any surprise when she removed her blouse and bra. Instead, I calmly directed her to lie stomach down on a towel while I caressed her back. She complied in silence, but for the first time I felt she was not just obeying a command. She had made a personal decision to go ahead with her therapy. And she had made it on her own.

When I finished, she waited while I lay down. Was it just my imagination, or did I feel a responsiveness in her touch that hadn't been there when she caressed my face two weeks before? I barely dared to hope. Was she becoming aware of her body and her sensations so soon? I had reason to be encouraged. Her movements were not carbon copies of mine, as they had been before. She even kept the stroking up a bit longer than I had. Had we already succeeded in releasing her from her fear?

When we were again dressed and sitting facing each other, I knew the lessons were far from over. She was the first to speak, and that was something of value. But what she said was mildly disappointing. "I still think it's wrong for us to have been half-undressed like that. People shouldn't do such things unless they're married."

"Why?"

She spoke hesitantly. In her family, sexuality was just not discussed. Sexual feelings were considered disgusting. I hoped that her courage in telling me this was an indication that she was beginning to question these ingrained beliefs. But she gave me no further clue as to her frame of mind.

When we separated, I reminded her that she should discuss these things with the therapist. I knew I would be doing that in our weekly conference. It was important that Angie had gone against her conditioning when she stripped to the waist. Maybe those taboos weren't quite as strong as she thought they were.

Before she left, I handed her a small package containing a series of vaginal dilators which she could use to prepare herself for the Pap smear. She thanked me and tucked them deep into her purse. I wondered if she'd dare to use them.

Our next session was to be a major one. The therapist had decided that we should at least discuss nudity and, maybe, even try to be nude together.

When Angie arrived, we embraced and then sat facing each other. "Angie, what do you think about nudity?"

She blushed, looking down.

"Does it embarrass you?"

She nodded.

I continued. "Why?"

"I've never seen anyone nude before. I've never even seen myself without clothes." The uneasiness I had assumed was a thing of the past was now back.

I took a gamble. "Nudity doesn't have to lead to sex, you know."

She nodded, hesitantly, but she didn't look at me.

"We don't have to take off our clothes, even though your therapist said she'd like us to. I promised you'd never have to do anything you didn't want to, and I meant it."

She looked up at last. "Okay. Let's get it over with."

I hesitated. Her switch was too sudden. I might have misinterpreted her meaning.

She rephrased her decision. "Let's get started."

I undressed in front of her, being careful not to force eye contact. When she began to disrobe, I turned away, pretending to be busy with a towel so she wouldn't feel I was watching her. As soon as we were both nude, I turned and had her stand some distance from me, holding my hands.

We followed the exercise to the letter, looking first at each other's faces, then moving our eyes slowly down each other's bodies. I was careful to spend the same amount of time on each area of her body, neither omitting nor over-emphasizing any one part more than another. When we were through looking, we hugged. It was a brief embrace, with no sexual overtones. She wasn't ready for that and, besides, I had told her nudity didn't have to be sexual. Fortunately, I felt no arousal, so there was no problem.

Still standing, I suggested that she ask about anything she might want to know. I didn't expect much. But she had obviously done some thinking since our last meeting.

She had many questions. By the time we were through, she had shown me the extent of her sexual innocence. "What are erections and why do boys have them? What happens when girls get aroused, since they don't have pe-nises?"

The hour seemed to fly past. As the session ended, Angie looked up into my face and smiled. "We're still naked!"

I nodded. "That's right. Have you been uncomfortable?"

"No." She casually glanced at our bodies. "It's neat. You're right. Nudity doesn't mean sex, does it?"

"That's right. It certainly doesn't have to."

"But it's fun, isn't it?"

Again, I agreed. It was time to dress and go our ways. As she embraced me and headed for the door, I wondered what miracles would take place before I saw her again.

She informed me as soon as we were settled into our next session that she had gone to her gynecologist and that he'd been able to get the speculum in and take a Pap smear. "He said everything looked fine in there. And it didn't hurt too much."

I took her hands in mind. "It's time we got to work. Don't you agree?"

She nodded. We were to try a sensate frontal caress, avoiding any genital contact. As I stroked her body, I was aware of how greatly she had already changed. She lay on her back, trusting that I wouldn't harm her. I kept my touch gentle, yet I was aware that she actually responded when I stroked her arms and shoulders, and when I touched her feet.

When it was her turn to caress me, I reminded her that she was to do anything that gave her pleasure, and not to worry about my reactions. She nodded and began. When she reached my genitals, she stopped. "I know I'm not supposed to touch you there, but would you let me anyway? I've never touched a penis."

"Go ahead. It's flaccid right now, of course."

"What does that mean?"

I explained the difference between flaccid and erect. "A penis gets erect when a man is sexually stimulated. Then it gets hard and a little stronger than it is when it's flaccid."

She pressed it lightly. "It feels funny. Sort of squishy." She touched it once more and then went on with her caressing.

When she finished, we once more sat facing each other, still nude. Again, we talked about what she had learned. And when she was dressed and ready to leave, her embrace reflected her greater confidence.

Our seventh session began with a grand announcement. "I've enrolled in night school." Angie was fairly bursting with excitement. "I'm taking a course in human sexuality. And I have lots of questions."

We spent some time discussing her lessons, but we still had enough left for the exercise the therapist had assigned. By now I was aware that Angie was changing quickly. I had a difficult time remembering the hesitant, frightened creature she had been when I first met her.

Her questions were directed toward her sexual problems. "If I have sex with you—sometime—won't it be painful? I'm afraid that if it hurts too much, I'll get scared and do something dumb."

I explained exactly what happens during intercourse, but she seemed preoccupied as I spoke. Finally, she burst out with a surprising statement—and another question. "You're going to have to show me. I just can't understand what you're talking about. But if you do, what happens if I fall in love with you?"

I smiled, aware of her animated face. This was the girl who only six weeks before had been so frightened she hadn't dared to say anything. Now she was declaring that we'd have to have intercourse. Still, she was not quite comfortable with the situation. "We won't have to 'do it' until you're ready. We might not do it at all. I said you'd never have to do anything you didn't want to. Remember? I think maybe someone else should be your first partner—someone more your age. As for pain, you don't have vaginal pain when you get examined by the gynecologist now, do you?"

She shook her head. "No, but . . ."

"There isn't any but. If you feel any pain during intercourse, it will be all in your head. If you really want to have sex, and you feel good about the man you're with, you shouldn't feel any discomfort at all. In fact, you'll feel very good."

She nodded, but still looked at me expectantly.

"Okay." I went on. "Let's talk about the possibility of your falling in love with me. It's all right if you do. After all, we know we're only going to be seeing each other for a short time more—until things are all right with you.

Besides, your therapist would help you work through any feeling like that, so you'd grow from the experience."
I took her hand. "I hope you could love me. I love you. You're a very special person. But just loving a person doesn't mean you want to marry them. That's quite a different kind of love, a kind you'll feel when you meet the right young man."

She smiled then—a clear, happy smile—and we continued on with our assigned exercise.

During that session and in the weeks that followed, she learned to take pleasure for herself. She learned how to awaken her body to pleasure and to enjoy herself as a sensuous human being. I helped her see how courageous she had been when she came to the therapist. She had made a choice for health. Many people who are as lost as she was are too afraid to reach out for assistance.

When we reached the session in which we began stimulating caressing, she was particularly alert. She had learned to relax, even when stroked, so she was able to enjoy her own arousal. When it came time for her to caress my body, I reminded her that even though I would probably get an erection, we didn't have to do anything about it. I wanted her to enjoy the feeling of seeing me aroused, even to feel my penis if she wanted to. But she did not have to assume responsibility for bringing me to orgasm. She was surprised. "But won't you be aroused just because I touch you?"

"Yes—and no. Your touch and caresses might get me aroused. But only if I want them to. And even if I get hard without intending it to happen, I'm still responsible. It's my erection, not yours."

Reassured, she completed the exercise. I didn't allow myself to get an erection. I felt she might be frightened by the change.

As she touched me, she remarked on how soft my penis felt. "It's so cuddly."

I accepted her remark, and she went on with the caressing. When the session was over, she hugged me very warmly. She was humming a tune as she headed down the hall to the therapist's office.

During the following session, we did a sexological examination. Her vaginismus was completely gone. Though she was hesitant when I inserted the speculum, she didn't wince. Soon she was relaxed and watching with a mirror as I pointed out the various parts of her genitalia.

That day she learned what parts of her vagina were sensitive, where her clitoris was, and how it worked. She was fascinated when she got a view of her cervix. "It's pretty, isn't it?" was her comment.

When we completed her examination, I lay down and she examined me. As she named the various parts of my genitals, she seemed particularly pleased with herself. "I've seen the pictures in books, and I memorized the names. But now I'm way ahead of the rest of the people in my class, aren't I? I'm getting to examine real genitals and not just pictures in a book."

Next we discussed how the penis enlarges. I explained about the chambers that get filled with blood. "Sometimes a man calls his erect penis a bone. But it isn't really. It gets soft again. The important thing to remember is that you don't have to do anything just because a man you're with becomes aroused."

"But what if he says I have to?"

I stood up. "Let's do some role-playing. It's time you learned how to say no."

We pretended to be sitting in her living room. I pushed close against her and gave her the age-old argument about how she was responsible for my arousal and she owed it to me to do something about it. She repeated what I had taught her. "No, I don't. It's your arousal, not mine. I'm not ready to have sex now."

"You don't love me, then," I continued, using the next argument a man might try. "If you loved me, you'd do it. If you don't, I'll be in real pain, and it will be your fault."

Again, she repeated what I had taught her, but I sensed more confidence in her voice. "That isn't true. I do love you. But you're not being fair. You say I must have intercourse with you to prove I love you. But if you loved me, you wouldn't force me. You'd be willing to wait until I was ready."

"Then you will do it with me sometime?"

"Maybe. If we both want it."

She sounded so confident, so mature, I could have kissed her right then. Instead, I continued with the role-playing. I suggested ways that she could say either no or maybe without angering her partner, and I gave her ideas that would help her negotiate for what she did want. She learned quickly, embellishing each explanation so I knew she understood what I was saying.

With ten minutes left of our session, I stood up. "What I really want is to hold you and hug you. I want to see how that feels to you."

She climbed back onto the bed and held out her arms. We lay facing each other, and she gave me a warm, wonderful embrace. Her lips against my cheek, she whispered, "Maybe sex won't be so bad, after all."

I kissed her lightly on the lips. "No, it will be fine. When the proper time comes." I knew my eyes were wet, and I saw tears glisten on her cheeks. How far she had come!

We kissed again, and then we dressed. I watched her as she walked lightly down the hall to the therapist's office. She was still a virgin, but she had changed. She was capable of feeling and expressing affection. She dared to accept me not only as her teacher but as her friend. Maybe I was the first friend she had ever had.

By the thirteenth session, she was asking about how she would feel if she became aroused. Would it hurt? If someone played with her clitoris, would it be painful?

The therapist and I anticipated these queries, and I was prepared to move ahead. Angie and I stripped and lay down on the bed. Gently, I began to stroke her clitoris, using plenty of oil on my fingers. When I felt she was aroused, I asked how she felt. "Does it hurt?"

"Oh, no. But I do feel kind of funny."

I took the hand mirror and held it so she could see her enlarged clitoris. "This is probably what your mother was talking about when she said something would get big and hard if you touched yourself. But you know now that it doesn't hurt. And it isn't that big, either, is it?"

She took the mirror in her hands and gazed into it in silence. "It looks like a tiny penis. Is that how penises look when they get hard?"

"A little bit. I think clitorises are a lot prettier. See for yourself." I rolled over so she could see that I, too, was aroused.

"It is big!" There was awe in her voice. "I don't think it would fit into my vagina."

"Look." I took the largest dilator she had used and held it next to my penis. Its diameter was considerably larger.

She began to giggle. "It isn't that big after all, is it? It just looks big because it's longer."

We lay for a moment in silence. Then I got up and returned to my chair. "Time for more talking. We'll hug again before you go home."

My next talk with the therapist was encouraging. "Angie's changed, hasn't she?" she began. "She's much more alive and alert. And she seems happier than when she first came to us. And more assertive. You're doing good things for her, Jerry."

"She still has problems, though." I felt pleased with the compliment, but I knew I was not solely responsible for Angie's improvement. "She told me she was still having problems at home, and she still isn't good at communicating with other people. I hope she isn't getting too locked into me. She needs to be free to expand her circle of friends. Those are things I can't do much about."

"No. But she's almost ready to tackle those problems. She just needs one more thing. She's still afraid to try intercourse with any of the young men she knows. I think you should be the first one."

I shook my head. "No. I've done a lot of thinking about it, too. Angie and I have talked about oral sex, anal sex, masturbation, paraphernalia like dildos, and even all kinds of abnormal sex. But we've also talked a lot about normal sex, which is the only kind that interests her. And she's ready for intercourse. Her vaginismus is gone. She's used a dilator bigger than most penises without pain, so she could take anyone she wanted. But I don't think I should be her first partner. Her first lover should be someone she chooses. A boy her own age. Someone she loves."

The therapist shook her head. "Not at all. Angie and I have talked about this a lot. Both she and I feel it should be you." She saw my head shake and hurried on. "Listen. She trusts you. She knows implicitly that you won't hurt her. Angie feels that you're her teacher. If she has sex with you, she won't feel that her virginity is gone. You've convinced her, Jerry, that when she really falls in love, she'll feel a lot more emotion. With the man of her dreams, it will be a totally different kind of experience."

The problem had been gnawing at me for the last few sessions. Was the therapist right? Was this the only right way for our sessions together to be ended? Angie had been so open. She had shared her fear of falling in love with me, and though I knew she loved me, I also knew she had never yet been "in love" with anyone. She had faced her deepest, innermost fears as she lay beside me. She had allowed me into areas of her psyche and permitted me to touch her body as no one had ever done before. We had developed a deep, abiding respect for each other. I honestly believed she would have done anything for me. Was that all this was? Did she feel she owed me sex? If so, I had failed.

I voiced my worry. The therapist smiled. "Not at all. You've made it very clear that she owes you nothing. Think it over. I know she's ready. If you agree, you should do it at the next session. You've been a good teacher. There isn't anything left for her to learn except to experience for herself that intercourse can be good."

I could sense Angie's nervousness at our next meeting. I wondered if she had changed her mind. "I know you've decided you want me to be the first." I spoke as we sat facing each other. "But if you change your mind, that's all right. And even if we go ahead and you want to stop, just say so. We don't have to do anything that doesn't feel right and natural to you."

She nodded, stood up, and began to undress. We lay together, fondling and caressing each other. I moved slowly, prepared for a sudden change in her behavior. If she grew frightened, I was ready to stop.

But she showed no great fear. Instead, she closed her eyes and let herself enjoy the caresses. When I felt she was ready, I gently penetrated her. But no more. I lay still. "Did that hurt?"

"A little." She didn't pull away.

I held myself still. "Let your body relax. You don't have to do anything. I'll push in again, slowly."

She nodded, and I eased farther in. I could feel her vaginal muscles grab, and suddenly I was all the way in. As that happened, she winced slightly. "Ouch!"

I started to pull back again, but she held me close. "No. It's all right now." The thing she had feared the most had barely hurt at all.

We spent the rest of the session in warm, sensuous lovemaking. It was an experience I will never forget. As she moved to increase her pleasure, I remembered the tense, frightened woman she had been such a short time ago. Now she had explored the last terror. Even intercourse could no longer frighten her.

Our last session was our closure. Angie looked lovely. She had lost weight over the months and had taken more care with her personal appearance. I knew she saw herself in a new light.

"Now you need to transpose what you've learned into a relationship with someone your age."

She nodded. "I'm still not sure about how to do it. I'm still not good at meeting people. I get embarrassed so easily. Couldn't we keep seeing each other until I got some more things straightened out?"

I shook my head. "No. I don't think that would be good for you. You've learned all you need from me. Now you need to spend time with people your own age."

"But what will I do?"

"What do you want to do? Didn't you say once you wished you could dance? Why not get into a singles square-dance club?"

She became animated again. "Yeah, I'd like to go camping, too. Do you think there's a camping group I could join?"

We discussed the many options she had—clubs she could join, situations she might encounter as she began to interact with her peers. We talked about her remaining fears and apprehensions. Was she comfortable with the ways to say no or maybe that she'd learned in our sessions together? What if she had a relationship with a young man her age and it turned out to be a disappointment? Could she accept such a failure and not have it affect her self-confidence?

We talked further, considering successes and failures, love and affection, closeness and intimacy. We discussed how far she had advanced in learning to communicate her wishes and what she needed to do to improve such skills.

And then, at last, we talked about our friendship. About what had happened to her during our time together. About how she had accomplished the goals she'd set for her sessions with me.

"I'll miss you, Angie. And I'll never forget you."

She met my gaze. "I'll miss you, too." She hesitated for only a moment. "If I need to talk to you again, can I?"

"Of course you can. Your therapist will pass on any message you want to give me. And I'll call you back. After all, you still have a lot of things to work through with her."

Angie nodded. "Remember how scared I was when I first met you?" She laughed at the memory.

"I was scared, too. I was afraid I couldn't help you. I wasn't sure that I might not frighten you more." I joined in her laughter. We had both been so uneasy, and now we felt like old friends.

She stood up and held out her arms. I stepped into her embrace. "Good-bye, my friend." I kissed her.

She returned my kiss. "Good-bye." Her arms tightened around me, and we hugged as we had never hugged before. And then, once more, she kissed me. "Good-bye."

She turned and walked to the door. With her hand on the knob, she paused. "Thank you—for everything."

I sat alone for a time after she was gone. I knew we would not see each other again, and I already missed her. But I knew, too, that I had learned as much from her as she had from me.

5

MARRIED WOMEN
Getting to Give

Most of us are taught from childhood that we must never be selfish. We learn little adages such as "It is better to give than to receive." As a result, many of us become afraid to take enjoyment from any of our acts—or to admit it if we do.

When we carry this attitude into our sex lives, we encounter problems. It causes us to think of sex as something we *give* to another. We become so preoccupied with giving the other person pleasure that we may discover, after we're through, that we've received little or no enjoyment ourselves. Most men, for example, operate during sex within a rather narrow range of acceptable behavior. They must always be in control. They must have strong erections. They must know the "right" techniques so they will be sure to give their partners orgasms. If they fail in any of these "essentials," they are devastated.

Women have their own requirements. They must give men pleasure, or at least let them have their own way. And they must do whatever is required to help their men become erect and expect nothing in return except a period of insertion—which is often far too short to be anything more than abrasive.

Does all this sound anachronistic—like a throwback to a previous generation? As far as present social standards are concerned, it is. But human bodies don't respond very quickly to changes in social standards. We may say that both women and men now have the right to sex for their own enjoyment. We may say that all "musts," or even "shoulds," are to be thrown out. But try to convince a human body that's given itself to another's pleasure for twenty or thirty years that what it's been doing isn't fair. Not an easy task.

Bodies evolve habitual responses that are not readily altered. The result is that, in many long-term relationships, anxieties may develop. Husbands and wives who have spent years thinking only of the other's pleasure become uneasy when they begin focusing attention on their own responses. They become genuinely concerned about what this is doing to their partner's satisfaction, for if one spouse is not satisfied, the other takes on the anxiety, assuming that selfishness has caused the failure.

Of course, not all married couples who have problems get into that particular bind. In some marriages, selfishness has been carried to the extreme. Often, it's the man who cares only for his own sexual release. He expects fellatio but refuses to perform cunnilingus, which he considers degrading. Even in nonsexual situations, such a person is likely to show little or no consideration for his partner. Such marriages need more than sex therapy.

Other married or committed couples fall into a pattern that is less obvious but just as damaging. For example, upon being seated in a restaurant the man will ask, "What would you like, dear?" The woman replies, "Oh, whatever you're having."

This sounds wonderful. Two caring people. But one of the two may actually be afraid of offending the other by showing any sign of disagreement. Often, it's the woman who passes the decision-making to her partner, making him responsible for satisfying her gustatory needs. If what is ordered displeases her, then it becomes his fault for making the wrong decision.

This kind of question and response can turn up in every area of human relationships. "What should we watch on TV tonight, dear?" "Oh, whatever you choose, darling." "Where shall we go this weekend?" "Wherever you'd like." Hold on there! If that's all the feedback I'm going to get, I might as well be alone!

Everyone needs feedback. If you and I are doing something together, I want reassurance that it pleases you. But I also want to be sure it doesn't offend you. Let's use a game of tennis as an example. If I serve the ball so hard and fast that you always fail to return it, you may not only be offended but may become bored as well, ending any possibility for a meaningful, pleasurable game—or any game at all. On the other hand, if my serve is such that you can usually return the ball and challenge me in getting it back to you as well, you'll be getting pleasure from the game, and so will I. The feedback I get from your reactions to my serves indicates to me how I should pursue the game—and the same is true from your point of view.

If I have sex with a woman, I need the same kind of continuous feedback. To learn how she truly feels about what's going on, I must receive a steady supply of signals from her. Logical, isn't it?

Logical. But far too few people act on that logic when it

comes to sex. Many women, probably because they are taught to ignore their own sexuality as they grow up, also learn to expect the man to know what will be most pleasing to them. To put it bluntly, such women expect men to be mind readers. The fact is, they are so alienated from their own sexuality that they truly don't *know* what feels good. They have to depend on someone else to tell them—or show them—what's best.

It's an old dilemma. The man is operating in the dark. He's exasperated because he gets little or no feedback. He has no way of knowing what will work and what won't. The woman is upset because she assumes that a man should instinctively know what to do to please her— but he isn't doing it! To overcome this impasse, the couple needs help. And so they come to a sex therapist.

In conventional therapy, there is a one-to-one relationship between client and therapist. Conversation is used as the vehicle of treatment, but the therapist gives as little advice as possible, allowing the client to reach insights that point the way to a cure. There is no physical contact involved.

If a man and wife come to a sex therapist or marriage counselor, they are usually interviewed together, then separately. Conventional marriage counseling and conventional "talk" sex therapy are really only effective if both partners are present.

In the early days of sex therapy, Masters and Johnson pioneered the concept of a male and female therapist team that would work with a married couple. Typically, the male therapist would first interview the man and the female therapist the woman. Then the four of them would work together for a few sessions.

At that point, they would reverse the procedure. The male therapist would interview the wife, and the female the husband. In some cases, more would come out during that opposite-sex interview than was elicited when therapist and client were of the same sex. This model for therapy was so successful that it became the standard in sex therapy countrywide.

Typically, the couple would meet with the two therapists in an office and, after a half-hour or so of talk, would leave the therapists and go into a private room for an hour of special exercises. These would include practicing sensate touching, body caressing, and other techniques that will be described more extensively later in this book. At the end of the allotted time, the couple would rejoin the two therapists and discuss how the exercises went. This general format would be continued throughout therapy.

But what happens if one spouse refuses to come in for therapy? What if the husband says, "It's your problem. You solve it." Working with only half the team is difficult. Much of the feedback derived from the private sessions is missing.

It is in such cases that a surrogate may be brought in. If a married woman comes in for therapy but her husband refuses to participate, then it must be determined whether or not she is a candidate for surrogate therapy. If possible, she is urged to tell her husband what is being considered and to ask how he feels about it.

In some cases, the spouse is required to sign a statement that he is aware his mate may be undergoing sex therapy with a surrogate and that he consents to it. Other therapists do not ask for such a disclaimer as long as the husband comes in and assures the therapist personally that he approves, or at least does not object, or doesn't care what happens as long as it's effective, or really doesn't want to know how the cure may be achieved, since knowing for certain that his spouse worked with a surrogate might harm their relationship.

Whatever the method used for gaining reassurance, it is only after the therapist is certain, beyond any doubt, of the husband's refusal to come in for therapy that the wife is matched up with a surrogate. Then, for the period of treatment, the surrogate becomes a true substitute spouse. The wife and the surrogate undergo the therapy treatment together, as a team.

Usually, after ten or fifteen sessions, there are enough positive changes in the wife to cause her husband to notice. At that point he may inquire as to what has made the difference. Once more, the wife is encouraged to try to get him to join her, or at least to talk to the therapist so that he can get complete answers to his questions.

Quite often, the husband then actually changes his mind, decides that he wants to share in his wife's treatment, and begins therapy himself. When that occurs, the surrogate's job is ended. The husband takes his place beside his wife, and the surrogate steps out of the picture. Sometimes, that transfer is delayed while the husband works with a female sex surrogate, who helps him reach the same level of development his mate has already achieved. Then both male and female surrogate bow out, and the couple continue on their own.

Frequently, the fact that I'm married is a big asset in my career as a surrogate. Single clients assume that I know more. Married clients feel safer with me, since they assume that I, like them, want to keep my marriage intact. They also seem to feel that I'll understand what goes on in a marriage more than a single man would. They know I'm committed to someone else, and that lends credence to my claim that we'll be working together on a strictly professional level.

I always tell my clients that I'm married. And because I can relate how my surrogate training strengthened my own marriage, my clients feel more certain that through what they learn with me they can improve their marriages, too. This makes it easier for them to transfer what they learn with me to their own relationships.

I've been asked if I have ever had to deal with a jealous husband. Truthfully, I have not. If a man knows his wife is working with a surrogate, it's usually because he realizes she needs special help. In such a situation, he accepts me as he does the therapist. When the therapy is over, it's the husband who usually benefits directly, since his wife has a new awareness of her sexuality.

In one instance, a married woman who was deeply in love with her husband came in for therapy because she wasn't enjoying their sex life at all. He had no concept of her needs, and she didn't know how to tell him what she wanted changed without hurting his feelings. After years of tolerating his way of doing things, she had finally decided to confront the issue. But he wouldn't even talk about it. Instead, he backed away from sex completely.

This finally resulted in arguments that were clearly leading to divorce. They were fighting one day when he blurted out, "You're the one who's frigid. Go get it fixed. I don't care how you do it. Just don't involve me!"

The thought had not occurred to her before. She was already aware that sex therapists existed and that some of them used surrogates, so she decided then and there to work with one of these substitute partners. But she was worried about two things. First, how would she tell her husband, without making him jealous or angry, that she had used a surrogate for sex therapy? And, second, how would she transfer what she learned back to him?

In marital sex difficulties, not all the problems are legitimately the wife's. Both partners do things that limit the pleasure they experience. This case was quite typical. The husband only approached his wife, only touched her or smiled at her or kissed her, when he wanted sex. She felt a need for more general closeness. She wanted to be touched and smiled at and kissed even when no sexual contact would follow.

When she came to us, she was convinced that if her husband would only show that little amount of caring, she would not only be ready for sex but would enjoy it when they had it. Then, she explained, loving him physically would be more than just a wifely duty. The problem was that when she attempted to make loving contact, he always interpreted her touching him as a prelude to sex. When he acted on what he was convinced was a clear signal and she backed off, he accused her of being frigid.

We began therapy together. Each session proved to me that here was a very sensitive, responsive woman. But as we advanced in the exercises, I could see that she was growing apprehensive. The truth was, she was frustrated. How would she get her need across to him when he refused to listen? What good was all she was learning if she couldn't communicate her new knowledge to the man she loved?

When, at the therapist's suggestion, she began touching her husband in nondemanding ways, he didn't seem to respond. After a time she complained about this lack of progress to the therapist, who urged her to continue the practice anyway. Then, some time later, her husband told her quite spontaneously that he liked the touching she'd been doing and subsequently began the same sort of loving, nondemanding caressing himself.

This was the beginning of his consciousness-raising experience. Over the following weeks, she began to suggest that they try some of the exercises she had done with me. Always, she presented the idea as something they might just try. She avoided any comment that might have been threatening to her husband. It wasn't "This is better than what we've done before," but rather "Since you liked that, you might like this, too."

In effect, this woman became an amateur therapist to her husband. By the time she was finished with her therapy and her work with me, she and her husband had built a firm foundation for renewing their marriage. Everything wasn't perfect yet, but they were both involved in actively doing something to make things better.

This case is fairly typical of the married clients whom surrogates deal with. Usually the wife comes in burdened with a sense of inferiority, feeling guilty because she isn't sexual enough. Often, she believes her sex fantasies are abnormal. Most of the time, these women try to avoid sex with their husbands because they get no pleasure from it. As a result, their men blame them for being frigid, and they blame their men for wanting only sex.

When we ask this kind of client why she doesn't communicate her true feelings to her husband, she replies that she doesn't know what to say or how to say it. Even though she may be well read and intelligent, she is usually lacking in sexual knowledge and does not have any skill in sexual techniques. Often, she's afraid that her husband will ridicule her, even if she's able to tell him what she wants.

Some of these women fear their husbands would suspect them of infidelity if they suggested acts that were new to their relationship. The end result is that they just can't discuss sex, even though they love each other and may be relatively well matched in other areas of their lives. The women are left to dream of a "good" sex experience and wonder what they would feel were they to have one. And the men are thrust into an endless guessing game. Will this please her and give her an orgasm? If not this, what else?

These women usually don't want to have affairs, and they don't want their husbands to have any, either. Nor do they want divorces. Many have the perspicacity to realize that the same thing would probably happen with a new mate. So they are left being dissatisfied when sex occurs, or they abandon it altogether rather than fight over it.

Some resort to alcohol or drugs. Others bury themselves in work, a new career, or advanced studies. Often, they end up being financially successful, sometimes even better off than their husbands. But they retain a hidden anger at their spouses, because the sex problems they have sublimated still nag at them.

The case of one wife I dealt with illustrates the compounding of problems that occurs when a woman sublimates her sex needs because she is unable to communicate them to her husband. Among other things, this wife delved into college studies with a vengeance. Not surprisingly, in a couple of years she earned a professional degree, got a high-paying job, and became financially independent. But her anger at her husband persisted, and now that she earned more than he did, he became jealous, critical, and even more sexually remote than before.

By now, however, she knew enough to recognize the value of therapy, so she announced she was going into sex therapy and wanted him to come along. He refused. It was her problem, he insisted. So she came alone. When she and her therapist decided she should use a surrogate, they also agreed not to tell her husband, since they were sure he would not be able to handle that knowledge.

I was brought in after several talk sessions, and it soon became obvious that this woman, whom I will call Lillian, had no understanding of how to have a good relationship with a man, even when sex was not involved.

With the therapist still in the room, Lillian talked about her work. She was an assertive executive, but she was considered a bitch by her male co-workers and a cold fish by the women. As she talked, we could see some of her problems. She felt completely subservient to all men and, therefore, could not conceal her hidden anger when dealing with them professionally. She could not make eye contact with a man when she spoke to him and, in fact, was so embarrassed in the presence of any man that it affected her work.

With women, her problem was different. She didn't know whether she was competing with every woman she met or if she ought to comply with their requests as an equal. She was never asked to go with the other women to lunch, nor was she included in their private conversations.

She related how the men at work often made double entendres or told dirty jokes in front of the other women in the office—and sometimes even made passes at them—but never involved her in such behavior. She finally admitted that she was at first proud to be considered above such "dirty" behavior but that she now felt left out and hated the feeling that she was an outsider.

During these talk sessions, she began to recognize some basic difficulties in her life. Her husband was a very social person. He loved people, and when they went out he was always the center of a friendly circle. But he made no attempt to assume his share of the responsibility for their marriage. She was growing more resentful of being left out of social life, even by her husband, while at the same time being expected to assume all the responsibility for the marriage.

When we finally began to have sessions without the therapist present, Lillian was frightened. She had never been allowed to accept herself as a sensual, sexual being.

Her strict puritanical upbringing still kept her from sexual pleasure. Many areas of her body, normally considered erogenous zones, seemed almost totally anesthetized.

She had never touched her own genitals, nor had she ever looked at them. She had been taught as a little girl not to be, or act—or feel—sensual. Now a wife, a mother, and a successful, attractive lady, she was still doing her best to repress her naturally strong sexual feelings. This attempt on her part was reinforced by her husband, who seemed to consider her a possession rather than a female partner.

As all this came out, the therapist and I agreed that Lillian did not require any sexual intercourse with me— at least not for some time. Intercourse was the last thing she needed now, for it would only have caused her to feel guilty, and she would not have derived any pleasure from it.

We spent the first fifteen or so sessions doing a lot of sensate-focused touching, beginning with hand caresses and continuing on to the rest of the body. By the end of that time, we were actually performing some genital caressing. At each session, I focused attention on getting Lillian's body to respond—in getting her to become aware of her reactions to touch. Little by little, we progressed. She began to accept her feelings of being sexual. She began to be more outgoing and assertive. She was no longer inhibited when we talked about sex.

By acting out various situations, she learned to ask for what she wanted. In touching, she learned to recognize her own personal reactions, so she was able to tell me how hard to press, when she preferred a lighter touch, and when she wished the touching to continue or cease. When we approached those areas of her body that had for so long been insensitive, she began by touching me in similar places and watching how I responded, while at the same time concentrating on how she felt as she caressed me. Gradually, as her hands developed more sensitivity, her body also began to respond when I touched her.

Each session was carried on with an admonition by the therapist that we make note of Lillian's growing sensitivity and then move on. What we were doing was nonsexual. But it didn't have to be nonsensual. We could both enjoy what was happening. If we got aroused, that was all right, too. The sensations could and should be appreciated. But I was to avoid any intimation that Lillian had to pursue her feelings. They were simply to be accepted and enjoyed.

By the sixteenth session, we had advanced considerably. Lillian was now aware of her sensitivity to touch in many areas that had at first seemed totally unresponsive.

We still hadn't had sex. But now it seemed to be a logical conclusion to the path we had been following, so I began working to help her become secure enough to ask for what she wanted. She also learned a number of sexual techniques. She was finally able to take the initiative and to recognize her own sexual feelings. The line had been drawn. She knew now that external assertiveness did not have to mean sexual aggressiveness, and that being sexy did not mean being promiscuous. Our working together had strengthened her feeling of security in her own sexuality.

In our closing session, Lillian and I settled a few unresolved conflicts that had developed. We expressed the fears we'd both had when we first began work together, and our joys at having resolved those fears while moving on to a constructive relationship in which we both learned. The therapist and I then proceeded to suggest methods that Lillian might use to transfer what she had learned to her relationship with her husband.

Sometime later, we received a letter from her. It turned out that she never did tell her husband about her work with me. What helped her marital relationship was what she had learned. The question as to how she had acquired her knowledge never came up.

Now, at last, she was able to respond to her husband's caresses. She felt herself to be an equal partner in their marriage, rather than merely a vessel for her husband's sexual demands. She dared to tell him, in a gentle way, what she wanted and what she didn't want. Because they had loved each other all along, and because that love was still strong, her husband appreciated what she had done in taking therapy. He was more amenable to her suggestions than before, and he did not feel threatened when she made them.

Was their marriage saved because of the therapy? As is true in most cases such as this, I don't know. Nor will I ever find out. It certainly appeared at the time that a relationship that had been close to breaking up was put back on solid ground.

But even if Lillian and her husband separated later, I know that the therapy Lillian underwent has been a positive thing in her life. With what she has learned about herself, she is in a far better position to establish a new, good relationship than she was before. Never again will she feel like an involuntary subject to be used for another's sexual pleasure.

Lillian, like most of my clients, deserves a tremendous amount of credit. She had the courage to seek help when she felt unable to cope, and, because of her commitment to living, she dared to do something about her life. Her motive at the start was a desire to be a better partner for her husband. She expected nothing for herself. But only when she learned to get pleasure was she able to give it. And that isn't surprising. How can anyone give something to another if they don't first know that what they're trying to give actually exists?

Sometimes, a wife in a deteriorating marriage will finally face the real problem and lay down an ultimatum: sex therapy—or divorce. One woman I worked with was in just such a situation but held off on that final demand. She simply told her husband that *she* was going in for sex therapy. She said nothing about a surrogate. She was sure he'd misunderstand and not be able to deal with the reality.

If a husband is aware that his wife is going to a therapist, but he knows nothing about her involvement with a surrogate partner, it's probably because he wouldn't be able to accept the idea of his wife working in this way with another man. But even without specific knowledge of how and why changes occur, he still reaps the benefits from her new, more sensuous behavior. And, often, this takes place because, after working with a surrogate, a woman has a clearer picture of what she likes during sex—and in a relationship with a man. She no longer has to merely hope her man will please her. She can now give him positive feedback, and he finally gets to abandon the guessing game.

One client told me that on her wedding night, when both she and her groom were total virgins, he nervously nibbled on her ear. She had been so ready to be turned on that it excited her. But after twenty years of marriage, he had still begun every sex session by nibbling her ear. She hated it. Yet she hadn't wanted to discourage him or hurt his feelings. She feared he'd never understand her changing her mind, since the ear nibbling had worked so well in the past. And, worst of all, he might think she'd only pretended arousal for all those years. But, in spite of her continued pretense, they had recently divorced, and now she wanted to be sure she would never get into a similar bind again.

"I hate giving directions when I'm making love," she explained. "I feel as if I'm furnishing a road map. What's the matter with men, anyway? Aren't they supposed to know how to please a woman?"

When I protested that men were just human, too, and couldn't read minds, she laughed. "Yeah, like the man I just dated. When we got into bed and I tried to tell him what I liked, he couldn't get it up. He finally got angry and informed me that he hated 'ballsy' women. 'Dammit,' he said, 'I know how to please a woman. I don't need some women's libber showing me how to be a man.'"

I had to agree with him on one point. When you're actually engaged in sex, it's never proper to discuss in any detail what is right or wrong, good or bad, about what your partner is doing or has just done. The subject should always be brought up in a totally nonsexual atmosphere. Maybe at the breakfast table, or on a ride to the beach. This way, no one can feel put down for an act that just occurred, or feel that what's being said is a form of instruction that must be obeyed.

If technique is discussed and agreed upon well before sexual involvement, then during the actual intimate moments you should each concentrate solely on your own pleasure. If, instead, you focus all your attention on your partner's satisfaction, you become obligated to continue doing it. And there's always likely to be a question in your mind as to whether or not you're doing it right. You are, in fact, performing. The only way to make sex a real pleasure is to enter into it because *you* enjoy what you're doing. In taking pleasure with another, you also allow that person to freely take pleasure. You get to give.

6

WHAT IS SEXY?
The Importance of Body Image

A friend once told me about a man who continually referred to women he knew as
"those gorgeous creatures." At first it sounded as if this
was the epitome of male chauvinism. But after talking
with him, my friend realized that this man really meant
what he said. He had the unusual ability to look past a
woman's physical appearance and deep into her soul,
where he inevitably found something that he recognized
as a sign of her beauty.

Apparently, he could do this with any woman. He derived great satisfaction from his relationships with
women, as well as gratifying the women he met. His tal-
ent was particularly valuable when he dealt with women
who were badly scarred, physically disfigured, or psychologically off balance, for he never failed to find something of beauty that made both him and them pleased
with their relationship.

The tragedy of many women is that they feel disfigured even when they're not. They see themselves as
being imperfect, and they are convinced that no man will
find them attractive. Some women cover this fear with a

patina of artificial sexiness designed to hide their true feelings about themselves. Others back away from any contact that might lead to intimacy.

Even women whom men perceive as beautiful are frequently victims of this false vision. Concerned with appearance beyond all reasonable requirements, they see even the smallest scar as a massive disfigurement. Often, they are also terribly aware of their own inner imperfections, angers, and fears. They sometimes harbor hostility for all men, who seem to be so fascinated by their outward sexy appearance and so disinterested in the unsexy, drab creature within. They make assumptions—based on their belief that sexiness is only skin deep—that interfere with their relationships even when there is no sex involved.

When a woman has such a warped self-image, she isn't easily convinced that her picture of herself is wrong. As we work with such a woman, we surrogates must be tactful, but we must also be honest. We have to find that inner beauty before we can be convincing, for the acute sensitivity of women who consider themselves ugly makes them especially aware of any pretense.

The problems created by this fantasy of disfigurement are well illustrated by my relationship with Estelle, who had undergone extensive surgery before she came to me. Her greatest fear was that, because of her body scars, no man would ever be willing to love her—that the scars would get in the way of his acceptance of her, just as they interfered with her own self-acceptance.

Estelle had become almost phobic about her appearance. She couldn't look at herself nude in a full-length mirror. She had strong sexual needs and desires, but she didn't dare risk a relationship because she knew how easily she could be hurt by rejection. She was convinced that even if she met a man who claimed to love her, he would run away in disgust when he saw how she looked undressed.

Deep down, she hoped her fears were unfounded. She had turned down a number of what could have been casual affairs, partly because she feared the rejection she was convinced would occur, and partly because she had moral objections to that kind of lifestyle. She decided on surrogate therapy because she hoped that in the safe, structured environment of a surrogate encounter she would have the option of backing away, if she grew too frightened, without losing what little she had of her self-respect. If her hired partner was too revolted by her appearance, and her worst fears were realized, she would have lost little more than money.

What she claimed she wanted was an honest opinion of her looks from a man who saw her nude for the first time. And she insisted that she was prepared for the worst. Both the therapist and I realized that this very perceptive and defensive woman would pay very close attention to my reactions. She would be alert to my body language as well as to any change in my facial expression. If I indicated any repugnance—even minimal—I would destroy any hope of salvaging her. The therapist was convinced that this lady was so close to despair, she might have a tendency toward suicide.

I was to help her see that even if she was as badly scarred as she believed herself to be, it was possible to get beyond her body surface and reach the true beauty underneath. Actually, this is a task that male surrogates are often called upon to perform—not necessarily because the client is truly unattractive, but, as already mentioned, because so many people, especially women, perceive themselves as being ugly and unworthy of love.

It was a heavy responsibility I carried to that first meeting. For that reason, the therapist kept close control of how I proceeded. Her client's life was literally at stake. We knew I would have to be perfectly honest and open with Estelle, and that I would have to deal with my own feelings as they came up. We could only hope that I would be convincing if I had to hide any revulsion I might feel.

Because Estelle's fears were so directly related to her body appearance, the therapist suggested that we have our first nude encounter early in the treatment in order to get past that trauma. We were to go up to a separate room, get undressed, and spend the entire hour looking at each other and at ourselves.

We were not to touch each other at all, except maybe for an initial hug. As we undressed, I was aware of an overpowering apprehension. I was reasonably convinced that I would not be repelled no matter how disfigured she was, but I was apprehensive of how she might interpret any involuntary reaction on my part.

And what if my unscarred body made her too aware of her own disfigurements? Not that I was any Adonis, but I'd encountered problems before when I faced the mirror beside a client. Would I be forced to talk about trivialities like my slight paunch or my crooked knees while my client stared at the scars from years of operations and remembered the pain they had caused?

Since Estelle suffered from such low self-esteem, wouldn't I add to her burden when she saw that I held myself in rather high regard? To put it bluntly, I was worried about how I'd be able to compare and contrast our bodies without being totally false in expressing my feelings. And if I let falseness creep in, wouldn't I only bring her more pain than she had endured already?

To my surprise, Estelle followed my lead and removed her clothes. Applying all the honesty I could muster, I casually glanced at her as I stepped out of my trousers. I was determined not to stare but, at the same time, not to ignore any part of her body. When I realized she was returning my gaze, I felt an awareness of her discomfort, for she wasn't sure how long she could look without annoying me, nor where she dared to focus her attention.

I asked her for a hug. She nodded agreement and stepped forward, her arms extended. I grabbed her hands, held them for a moment, and then pressed my body lightly against hers in what I hoped felt to her like a warm, genuine embrace. I certainly didn't feel aroused, and I really didn't sense the warmth I had hoped for. But I realized that I wasn't giving off any feeling of warmth, either.

I stepped back, ready to proceed with the visual exploration. "Let's start with our hair, looking at each part of the other's body, moving our attention slowly down to the feet. Don't linger anywhere, and don't skip anyplace. We want to see something of each other, something that will tell us what kind of people we are. Okay?"

She nodded and we began. Rather to my surprise, it started out very well. We enjoyed each other's eyes and what we saw in them. Estelle remarked that she had never before been quite so aware of the color of a person's eyes. The success of our beginning made both of us feel more comfortable as we moved our eyes downward.

When I focused on her chest, my first reaction was shock. Where was the terrible scarring I had anticipated? True, she had obviously sustained extensive surgery. I've worked with other women who had undergone mastectomies that truly did leave horrible scars, but Estelle's were well-healed, thin lines across her chest. They were many, but they were not the disfigurements I had been led to expect. I saw none of the horrible, ugly, open wounds that Estelle had described to me and her therapist.

She seemed reassured by my reaction, for I showed no revulsion, since there was nothing to arouse it. Pointing to a scar that was still pink, she spoke. "That was my last operation. It was performed in Denver."

I nodded and waited. She continued, pointing to each scar in turn and telling me a bit about the operation. I accepted her information without comment and with no show of surprise or shock. I knew where the horrible scars were. They were hidden deep in her heart and mind, and until she could heal those inner wounds, she would never be able to see her own body as it truly was.

We spent a good twenty minutes discussing her various operations, moving easily down to her stomach, where more cleanly healed scars attested to additional hours on the operating table. We talked a little about her stomach being a bit soft and "poochy," but she acknowledged that she could do something about that if she wished to.

We continued the visual tour and discussed what we liked and what we disliked about our own bodies and each other's. Now we were able to have another hug, this time with real warmth and some affection. We sat down on the bed and for the rest of the time talked about our lives. She remained relaxed and was able to speak honestly about the pain she'd endured and to express, possibly for the first time aloud, how she really saw herself and why she felt so ugly.

She was obviously relieved to see that I was genuinely interested in what she had to say. I had not recoiled nor shown the disgust she had expected. In a sense, she had already received what she had wanted, for there had been no fraud in my response to seeing her. She admitted that I was the only man except for her doctor who had seen her body since her surgeries. She made no attempt to conceal her relief that I had not backed off in horror.

I left that session with glowing optimism.

But for all of that first success, her treatment with me failed. As Estelle got into her talk therapy, her past misfortunes surfaced. She had been terribly abused psychologically as a child. And as she matured, men had taken advantage of her. With each new mistreatment, her self-image had received another blow. She resented the way men had dealt with her, and she hated herself for letting herself be so misused.

Each time we'd begin a breakthrough, Estelle would accuse me of using her. She reminded me that I was only with her because I was paid for it, so she couldn't trust anything I said. Eventually, she became convinced that I was there only for my own pleasure. She decided that the therapist was in business to provide me with women— that the two of us were in collusion to take her money. With each session, her paranoia grew.

Finally, we had a three-way talk session that helped me feel better. I was able to thank Estelle for all she had taught me, for she had given me a greater understanding of the real inner pain and suffering a human can endure. And Estelle, in a last-hour recall of that first meeting, was able to admit that there had been moments when, as she put it, "we seemed to be getting somewhere."

I had to be content with that. Knowing her background made it easier for me to accept my failure. But I think I got the greatest lift from overhearing her last words to the therapist. She spoke apologetically. "I hope you understand. I'm going to try someplace else."

We two professionals who had just failed met each other's eyes. There was still hope. Maybe someone else would succeed. If we hadn't helped her cure herself, we had at least not destroyed her hope. Estelle was not giving up. That, certainly, was a plus.

When we fail, we have to go on to other challenges. It's

that way in every field of human endeavor. In the years that followed, I encountered many other women whose basic problem was a poor self-image. It's a devastating malady. Not only can it block attempts to reach self-acceptance, it can destroy natural sexiness and replace it with an image that no one can accept. What's more, self-image is often intricately woven into a person's perception of others.

Many women base their perception of themselves on how men react to them, especially during sex. They assume that if they are truly sexy and desirable, a man will have an erection as soon as he sees them nude, or as soon as they've touched him. In such a situation, a woman's decision regarding her own value is dependent upon the state of her partner's penis.

Sometimes, even her ability to achieve orgasm becomes psychologically tied to the size of her partner's penis. The mystique surrounding a big penis may give a woman the idea that only a large organ can be truly satisfying. This is not true. The vagina is very adaptable. It can contract and expand as needed. As long as the p.c. muscles are strong, penis size should not be critical in sexual pleasure.

Donna, a client I worked with shortly after my relationship with Estelle, made me aware of how often women link the sexiness and desirability of a man to the size or shape of his penis, and how damaging to happiness such an association can be.

Donna had been married twice. She'd had a great sex life with her first husband, but nothing else had worked for them and so they broke up. With her second, everything was reversed. She got along well with him in every area except sex. She subsequently became very dissatisfied with her life in general, and several years of conventional therapy had not helped her. Now she was living with a man whom she loved, but their sex life was not good.

Our first session was rather ordinary. We did focused caressing of hands, face, feet, and hair, and in the process became very comfortable with each other. We enjoyed the sensate touching, and we discovered that we both liked the way the other kissed.

In our second session, we were to do body imagery. In surrogate work (and in sex therapy), we find that sexually dysfunctional people often do not like themselves or their bodies, even though they may be perceived as being perfectly acceptable by others. Often, by discussing size, shape, scars, fatness, skinniness, hairiness, and anything else that we think might be disliked, we relieve tension and alleviate the fears a client may have. This self-examination is also a wonderfully gentle way to ease into nudity and to separate nakedness from sex.

When I asked Donna how she felt about getting undressed, she answered, "Fine. I'm anxious to see the size of your cock."

Such a response might work on a first date with someone (though I doubt it), but it certainly did me no good. I felt my ego ebbing away onto the floor. What if I didn't measure up? Why the hell was she so interested in my cock, anyway? She wasn't here for stud service.

My mind rushed to save me from my nervousness. Why get so upset by one stupid remark? I didn't even know what she really meant by it. Besides, here was my masculine concern about penis size rising up as if I were an inexperienced kid. I knew that most men think they're smaller than they really are. It's because we look down at our cocks. Try looking into a mirror, I said to myself. You'll feel better.

Usually, I undress in a jiffy. But this time I had difficulty moving. Annoyed at myself, I hurried to take off my trousers and put them on a chair. There would be no close embracing, no genital caressing. I was reasonably certain I wouldn't have an erection, so she'd get little chance to evaluate how big I really was. We all know (don't we?) that a flaccid penis is no indicator of erect size.

Despite my nervousness, the session went well. We undressed and looked at each other's bodies, discussing what we liked about ourselves and the other person. Then, with the positive aspects clear in our minds, we continued on to what we didn't like about our bodies. We talked, discussed, looked at each other, laughed, and recalled incidents that affected our self-images. Nothing more was said about my penis.

In fact, nothing more was said for the next four or five sessions. During the eighth meeting we were to do the sexological examinations, and for that purpose we had a gynecologist's table in the room, stirrups and all. Donna went first. Using a mirror, I let her see into her vagina. She was delighted at how pink and pretty it was. She asked questions and I tried to answer them as best I could, making notes of anything that might be helpful to her therapist.

Then it was my turn. As I climbed onto the table, I was reminded again that this is the position required by every gynecologist when he examines a woman. It's necessary if he's to see into her vagina. But how awkward that traditional pose makes a patient feel! There she lies, with her legs bent and spread. She's vulnerable, helpless. I've experienced that same helpless vulnerability every time I lie down and let a client begin to examine me.

As Donna began to study my body, I started my usual patter. "Males and females are far more alike than we often think they are. See that line down the middle of my scrotum? That's the *raphe,* the line where the two halves of the labia have grown together in the male when it was still an embryo. In the female, they remain separate and the vagina forms between them. And the clitoris is formed from the same stub that becomes the penis in the male. Only, in the male embryo, the urethra is routed through the stub, while in the female it remains alongside it."

Donna listened in seeming fascination as she continued her examination. She felt my testicles, the "balls" inside the scrotum, carefully noting the shape and texture of the sac. Then she moved her hands up the shaft of the penis as I named each part. The coronal ridge, the frenulum, the scar from my circumcision.

At this point, she put some oil on her hands and began to stroke the shaft. That wasn't quite in the plan for the day. I was about to suggest that she stop when it occurred to me that she had already expressed curiosity about my penis size. After all, she'd been very patient since her declaration during our first visit that she wanted to see how big my cock was.

I decided to let her continue—in the interest of science. Besides, what she was doing felt wonderful.

When I was fully erect, she exclaimed gleefully, "That's beautiful! That's gorgeous!"

She couldn't have said anything more desirable. I can tell you honestly that nothing gives a man more gratification than telling him what a beautiful penis he has. Feeling pleased as punch and knowing my ego was rising far higher than my penis, I asked her why she was so interested in my size. I don't know quite what I expected in response, but what I got was the beginning of her therapy.

Her first husband had had a large penis, she told me, far larger than mine, and sex with him had been wonderful. Her second husband's was small. Smaller than mine. With him, sex had been very bad. Now her present boyfriend had an enormous penis ("two or three times" bigger than mine) and it was "just awful." When it was flaccid, it rested on his stomach like a big, squishy flab, and when it was erect, it was so big she couldn't do anything with it. Oral sex was out of the question, as was anal intercourse. "What can I do with a guy like that?" she asked, her voice echoing her despair.

I remembered a comment a gay friend of mine had once made when referring to a lover's enormous penis. "With a cock like that, all you can do is hug it and cry." But though the memory made me smile, I knew it would not console Donna. I remained silent. When she told me that her boyfriend was often impotent with her, I was glad I'd kept the joke to myself.

Instead I began to ask about her responses. "What kinds of things did you do with your second husband? Usually, a small penis isn't that important. The p.c. muscle is very adaptable."

Her answer surprised me. She had actually done very little during sex in either of her marriages. She had just accepted what her first husband did for her, and she'd attributed the pleasure she got to his penis size. In fact, she put so much emphasis on penis size that she'd never enjoyed good sex with her second husband. Now she was well on the way to ruining her relationship with her boyfriend because his penis was not her ideal, either. She had never taken any responsibility for her own pleasure. If sex was good, she assumed it was because her partner had the right-sized penis. If it was bad, he didn't. And since mine now seemed the perfect size, sex with me, she decided, would naturally be perfect. What a simple way to dump responsibility!

Fortunately, in this one encounter, so much came out

about how Donna actually felt about herself that there was material for many talk sessions with her therapist.

During the weeks that followed, Donna learned that she had made an unconscious decision to accept physical attributes as the obvious cause of sex pleasure or boredom. It never occurred to her that she had the ability to control her responses or to try different things with different people. In her therapy sessions she learned that organ size was of such minor importance that she would have to look elsewhere for blame if sex wasn't good for her.

Gradually, Donna came to see that she was following a similar pattern in all her relationships. If things went well between her and her friends, they were being nice. If things went badly, it was because they were unkind and to blame for the difficulties. Donna had never accepted responsibility for her own actions, either in sex or in day-to-day life. Now the path to solving her problem was opened, and all because my penis was "the perfect size."

That isn't to say my penis did the job. But her judgment of it gave us a wonderful insight into her character that we might not have gained in any other way.

The tendency Donna showed to consider sexiness a function of the body is common. We experience the effect of that attitude every day. Women with big breasts are sexy. Men with big bulges catch the eyes of passing women on the street. Most men and many women, when asked to describe sexiness, talk about physical attributes. Yet the clues all around us point to a deeper base for human sensuousness.

In marriage, many couples complain that sexiness vanishes after a year or so, and often they're right. It's easy to say that this is caused by one or the other's gain in weight. But body size often isn't what has changed. What's different is the way they *think* about each other—

and themselves. How often does a busy housewife or businesswoman greet her husband with the allure she was careful to exude while they were dating? Does she even think of him—or herself—as being sexy anymore? And the husband? Doesn't he fall into the same trap? His wife becomes a mother, and he forgets that she's still the same woman he longed for so passionately before they were married.

Sexiness is in the mind. Some of the most sensuous clients I have had were not physical beauties. It's a serious mistake to attribute sexiness to appearance. My experience with Donna finally focused attention on that fact. When I thanked her during our closing session, my appreciation was sincere.

While we're on the subject of how the penis affects a woman's feeling of sexiness, or her evaluation of herself and her role in relationship to a man, I recall two other incidents that led to a greater understanding of the deepest recesses of a client's mind. These deal with the belief many women have that a man either does or should respond to the presence of a sexy woman by having an immediate erection. In one case, my arousal was instantaneous and inappropriate to the situation. In the other, my control was appropriate for my role as surrogate, but my lack of arousal brought a major problem to light.

I had been working with Gladys for ten or twelve weeks, making little progress, when we were told to go into a separate room (away from the therapist) and let her do whatever she wished for our hour together. She was to be assertive, to ask for what she wanted, and to be as explicit as possible. We had only one restriction. No intercourse.

As we undressed, I couldn't help but notice that Gladys was wearing the sexiest lingerie I'd seen in a long time. What's more, in a totally uncharacteristic manner, Gladys seemed to be flaunting herself as she disrobed. Knowing how reserved she usually was, I tried to convince myself that this was simply my reaction to the great lingerie. But my penis would have none of that. By the time I was nude, I had a full erection. Since I didn't have even an empty coffee cup in which to hide it, I simply turned and faced her.

As she saw my erection, Gladys dropped the sexy, jovial demeanor she'd had. Her mood suddenly turned sour. Her lips in a tight thin line, she walked silently over to the bed and sat down.

I couldn't ignore the fact that my erection was the cause of her displeasure, but I decided to wait for her to put the situation into words.

She said nothing, however, so, after a few minutes of silence, I spoke up. "You're not helping yourself by just sitting there. Why are you angry? If you can't talk to me, then get dressed and go talk to your therapist."

"Damn you!" I felt the force of her anger in her words. "We're here for my benefit. I'm paying for this! But you're just like all men. You have that big hard-on and now I'm going to have to do something about it, whether I want to or not. I haven't even touched you yet. What the hell did I do to get you that hard?"

For a brief instant I held back, aware that I was the surrogate and I should remain calm. But my irritation was too great. "Hey! I don't know what kind of power you think you have, but let's get this clear. This is my erection! I take full responsibility for it." I was upset now. "I enjoy having a hard-on, and you didn't necessarily give it to me. What's more, you don't have to do anything about it, so why the hell are you so upset?"

Even my ridiculous appearance didn't affect her. Her face still red with anger, she stood up. "Because you're all alike. All you men ever think about is your cocks.

You . . ." She sputtered before she continued. "You're a surrogate. You're supposed to be different. You're not supposed to make me feel guilty." As she finished, she dropped once more to the bed and covered her face. I could see that she was crying.

I sat down beside her and took her hands in mine. She dropped her head on my shoulder and continued crying. Five minutes later she looked up, her cheeks still wet with tears. I felt totally drained. Even my erection, the cause of this emotional outbreak, had finally faded. I stood and drew her to her feet. "May I hug you?"

She responded by putting her arms around my neck. When our lips touched, she pushed her tongue into my mouth and ground her pelvis against my now-very-soft penis. She was showing all the signs of sexual arousal, yet she was still angry and hurt.

I stepped back and we sat down again, still holding hands. As we talked, her anger once more erupted. All of her sexual life she had given to men to satisfy their needs because she'd felt responsible for their arousal. She knew she was considered a good partner, because the men she was with were always satisfied. But none of them seemed to notice that she received no pleasure herself.

I began to suspect part of her problem. Later, when I talked to the therapist, I was able to present a fairly complete picture of the reasons why Gladys had trouble with her romantic relationships. She gave double messages to the men she encountered. When she kissed me, for example, I could have assumed that she was very horny, ready for intercourse. However, I knew she wasn't. I knew she was still angry and feeling sorry for herself. So I realized that what she really wanted from me was closeness, nurturing, understanding. But she had a picture of male–female relationships that obligated her to act sexy even when she didn't feel aroused.

There were other aspects to her problem, and some of them came out that day. She honestly believed that she was solely responsible for the erections men had when they were with her, and she didn't recognize that she was giving her partners messages she didn't intend. Her mind was in one plane but her body in another.

This is a problem that some women have. A woman who wants to be cuddled and held may approach her partner and kiss him. The man may interpret this move as an overture to sex, so instead of getting hugs and tenderness, she gets intercourse. She therefore concludes that sex is all men ever think of, and her husband or partner is confused because she isn't satisfied, even if she's had an orgasm. As far as he can see, she initiates the sex but never seems to be happy with it.

The pathetic irony of this situation is that men have the same need for emotional support. Many of them admit they want tenderness but feel deprived of the nurturing touch because they, too, seem to send out sex messages when they're really asking for closeness.

With Gladys, we were able to detect the problem early enough for the therapist to be of help. In the sessions I had with Gladys after that breakthrough, we worked on teaching her better ways to show her feelings. By the time she left us, I believe she finally knew for certain that each person is responsible for his or her own sexual response. Never again will she feel coerced into "doing something" about an erection just because some man she's with has one. This insight into her image of men as being sexually demanding and of herself as being required to satisfy that demand came because I had an erection when it was totally inappropriate. Dealing with it, we unearthed information that would not have surfaced in any other manner.

In the second case, it was my lack of an erection that

led to the breakthrough. After five sessions with Helen, we were ready for the frontal sensate-focus caress, including a casual touching of the genitals. We were not to spend any more time on the genitals than on any other part of the body. Our main aim was to recognize the skin as a powerful sex organ.

I began by caressing Helen, since she chose to receive first. Beginning at her forehead, I caressed her gently, using powder on her body. I let myself enjoy the feel of her soft skin and the roundness of her curves. This was a part of the therapy that I found particularly pleasurable.

After twenty minutes I paused, she sat up, and we hugged. Then I lay down and she began the sensate-focus frontal caress on me. When she got to my penis, she casually stroked it, paused, stroked it again, and then moved on to my legs. But she did not continue. She stopped, sat down on the bed beside me with her back turned, and seemed to freeze.

"Is something the matter?" I half sat up.

She didn't answer immediately. I was ready to press my question when she suddenly spoke. "I don't know what the hell I'm doing here. No wonder no one finds me attractive or sexy. I realize some men might not get turned on by having their penis stroked, but you . . ." She faced me, her expression stern. "You're a surrogate. You should be able to get it up whenever you want to. If I can't turn you on, how can I expect to turn on anyone else?"

The irony of the situation! Now I was in trouble because I *didn't* have an erection! But, then, Helen had a different problem from the one that bothered Gladys, even though they both felt responsible for a partner's arousal. To Gladys, an erect penis meant that she had to perform to satisfy. To Helen, an erect penis was a sign of approval, proof that she was worthy. If a man didn't have an erection, she was convinced she was undesirable.

Once more, the condition of my penis served as an entree into a client's mind. I can't give my particular anatomy credit for this. Helen had encountered similar responses all of her life, but her previous partners hadn't been in a position to evaluate their state of tumescence as an indication of a psychological problem. As in the previous situations, the client's self-image influenced how she responded to my physical reactions.

Helen didn't know what it was that turned a man on. She thought it might be beauty, or big breasts, or sound, firm buttocks, or a narrow waist. When I tried to explain that only I was responsible for my erection, and that I had decided not to have one, she didn't at first understand.

It was weeks before she finally recognized that I had been enjoying her touch for what it was meant to be— warm and loving, but not sexy. With the help of the therapist, she began to see that arousal is a state of mind. And so is sexiness. She learned that her perception of herself was more important than what she assumed others thought of her.

She came to realize that no one can define sexiness by describing shape of body or style of dress or even manner of walk. Sexiness is a personal thing—a reaction, a chemistry—between two people. The feelings, emotions, and physical skills that go into making up this ambiance are highly individual. They originate in the mind, not in the genitals. A woman might seem sexy to one man and not to another. But she should *feel* sexy herself no matter how the men she meets react. You can't give love unless you feel lovable. You can't even approach someone unless you first feel approachable.

I have mentioned body image in two very different ways. In the cases of Gladys and Helen, I dealt primarily with how we can often project onto bodies what should be mental and emotional responses. When I spoke of Donna, I dealt with self-image as it applies to people who may actually have some physical scars or disfigurements.

Of course, one doesn't have to be actually disfigured in order to have a poor body image. On the contrary, from time to time in my career I've had exceptionally attractive women as clients, women who could have passed as beauty contest winners or Las Vegas showgirls. It's surprising how often such a woman feels that her beauty is a curse, that she succeeds in life only because of her physical attributes, that men have never taken her seriously or learned to appreciate her for who she is.

When I asked one stunning client what she wanted from a man, she said, "I would like, just once, for a man to look at my eyes when he talks to me instead of at my tits." While a youngster, this woman was Daddy's little girl and could get away with anything. As she grew older, her beauty continued to make life easier for her, but she felt that, in most cases, other women mistrusted her and saw her as a threat where their men were concerned. Her good looks were *her* "disfigurement"—and she needed as much help, counseling, and understanding as any of her physically flawed sisters.

7

AN ASIDE TO MEN
Passions and Pitfalls

A day doesn't pass when I'm not reminded of how ordinary a man I am. I've played almost every role society has ever demanded of the masculine sex, and some that most men and boys avoid.

I was a sickly child. When I was nine years old, I was raped by my baby-sitter, who held me down on the floor and forced me to perform cunnilingus on her. The shock of that experience was so great that for years I pushed it out of my consciousness. Fortunately, a loving and gentle friend took me under her wing when I reached my teens and taught me the pleasure of an act that had been only frightening to me as a child.

I was a son and a brother. As I grew, I was a choir boy, a boy scout, an average student, a teenage sex fiend, an athlete, a sailor, a disenchanted veteran, a wanderer, and a traveler. I was, at various times, both a blue-collar and a white-collar worker, as well as a professional. Eventually, I became a husband, father, lover—and a sex surrogate. I have been tough, macho, boastful, and chauvinistic. I have also been weak, warm, tender, loving, and understanding. I can be shy and reserved, and I'm not afraid to cry when I'm hurt or feel misunderstood. But I can find myself suddenly outraged or worried because my masculinity appears to be threatened. I can run the gamut from wild delight to deep despair. I know some things about life and am abysmally ignorant about others.

Despite the likelihood that I've had experience with more women than the average man in our society, I've learned only one thing for certain about them through all my relationships. It's that there's no such thing as being able to understand "women." Each woman is unique. But, then, that shouldn't come as a surprise. Every man is unique, too, even though we have many things in common.

When I was a weak child, I often wept because my peers were cruel to me. I only wanted what most boys wanted—to run and play active games and be accepted as one of the gang. But I didn't fit in like most of the others and was taunted and badgered because of it.

In my early teens, a wonderful teacher took an interest in me and transformed me into a powerful and agile athlete. When I joined the Navy, I wanted everything that spoke of masculinity. I wanted to be a boxer, a wrestler, a commando. I felt so strong and indomitable that I pictured myself winning the war singlehandedly. Fortunately, the Navy needed electrical engineers more than heroes, so my fantasies were never fulfilled. I stood on the sidelines and watched other men become heroes or cowards, and I began to wonder what it was that could make one man respond with courage and another with fear.

When I left the service, I studied psychology, hoping to find some answers to my questions. But they were few and far between. What I got, instead, were theories and hypotheses. There were experiments and researches. And there were books—many wonderful books that held stories of life. However, nothing pointed the way to the solutions of mankind's—and my—problems. So I decided to just live a bit.

For three years I traveled around the country. Part of the time I lived as a bum on skid row, but I also worked as a farmhand, a riding instructor, and even a gambler. My two main objectives were to drink anything that could be poured from a bottle and to screw anything that wore skirts. Eventually, I met a wealthy girl and lived briefly like royalty on Nob Hill in San Francisco. I also shared my life for a time with an actress in Chicago, a prostitute in North Carolina, a shopgirl in Arizona, and a model in Kansas City.

I met my wife-to-be at a party. She was the girl in a flowered dress, with great legs and a wonderful smile. She had been on her own since she was very young, and the fact that such an independent person could see anything in me was exciting. I found I didn't want to be apart from her, and I realized that all the sex I had experienced over the years meant nothing, because it had been mechanical—a physical release of tension. With her, I began to see that all my life I had been searching for intimacy.

Six months later, while walking through a Chicago snowstorm, I decided to move to California and put my life together. I had no money and no job waiting, but I realized I had to take my fiancée with me. I planned to stay with relatives until I got settled, and I pictured myself sharing Christmas with them while she sat alone in her walk-up kitchenette apartment. I couldn't bear the thought of leaving my lovely girl so isolated.

At three A.M., I wound up at her apartment and

knocked so hard on her door that her roommate was ready to call the police. Fortunately, I convinced her I wasn't crazy, and she at last let me in. I dashed into the bedroom, telling her to get up and pack and to call her boss in the morning and quit. "We're going to California. Please, take a chance on me. I want you to meet my family, and then, if you're willing, we can get married."

I still wonder at her courage. She was ready when I came to pick her up the next day. In California she met my family, and we were married on December 23, my parents' anniversary. She became the daughter they had never had, and they became the parents she had never known.

My wife worked for a few years, but when our first child was expected, she decided to quit and be a full-time mother—a decision she has never regretted. I returned to college to earn my engineering degree. After we bought our first house and settled into being a conventional family, I continued on with my schooling, taking night classes. I finally completed pre-med, only to learn that I was too old to be accepted into medical school. So I moved into the field of psychology, working toward a Ph.D. I studied hypnosis and began to work as a hypnotherapist. In that capacity, I acquired many female clients, but I knew that as long as my relationship with these women was professional, I would have no problems at home.

Through my female clients, I learned a great deal about women and about myself. Besides learning conclusively how damaging incorrect sexual information can be, I learned that we all have limits and that we have no reason to be ashamed of that.

Later, as a sex surrogate, I discovered *my* limits when I worked with a client who was close to the end of conventional therapy. Everything was going well for Cora except her sex life. She claimed to feel unfulfilled, even though she was capable of orgasm and had had almost every sexual experience she could wish for. But she didn't enjoy sex. She felt that it was too routine, and she was bored with the repetition. There must be something more, she insisted. Her therapist, feeling she could benefit from a surrogate, called me in.

We knew that, for her, sex was very localized. Only when she was extremely aroused did sensation move from her genitals to the rest of her body. The therapist had tried to explain to Cora that the solution to this condition lay in her own mind, but she was unable to really understand what that meant. Even her orgasms, Cora insisted, were not powerful enough or of long enough duration. What she really wanted was to have her "brains screwed out." She wanted sex with a superstud, a macho man to end all macho men. She wanted a partner who could stay with her for as long as she wished and bring her to heights of sexual pleasure never experienced before.

Both the therapist and I were convinced that her dream was impossible to realize. Cora was dumping all responsibility for her sexual pleasure on her partner. But, at the same time, there is always an exception to every rule. Maybe, for Cora, the dream could become a reality.

After extended consultation with the therapist, I agreed to try to play the macho role for Cora. If I could get her to respond as she fantasized, maybe I would get some insight into why this dream was so important to her. We both knew that Cora didn't need super sex. But she had to be shown that. And I hoped I was the right man for the job.

I abstained from sex for several days before this big session, and when I showed up, I was dressed in my most macho clothes. I had psyched myself up, too. I had built up an elaborate fantasy of what I was going to do and how I would do it. I don't mind admitting that by the time I reached the therapist's office and went off with Cora, I was ready. I was convinced that I'd show her what a real man was like.

Cora, too, had been anticipating the session, so we had little need for foreplay. I can't remember ever being harder, nor can I recall being with a woman who was aroused so quickly. It was with a feeling of triumph that I began intercourse.

At first, the emotional high gave me extra strength. I pumped and banged and humped. I breathed deeply and contracted my p.c. muscles. I tightened my anal and stomach muscles. And I pumped and banged some more.

Cora was responding just as I had expected in my dreams. She screamed and bucked and groaned, and each movement she made gave me added encouragement. But after ten minutes (which seemed like ten hours), my back began to give out. I wasn't having as much fun as I had anticipated. What's more, Cora's bucking and screaming had stopped. I took this to mean that she had already come, and I felt somewhat relieved. But since she hadn't volunteered that information, I decided to continue and not ask any awkward questions. If she wanted me to stop, I was sure she'd tell me. I expected to hear the magic words very soon.

Two or three minutes later, I was close to collapse. Without losing a stroke, I bent closer and looked deep into her eyes. There was emotion there, it was true. But not the kind I needed. She was bored. Totally and completely bored.

Automatically, I slowed down.

"If you want to continue, you can. It feels pretty good."

Something snapped. "Feels pretty good! Jeezus! I could be tickling your ear and getting some rest. That would feel good, too. What the hell do you want, anyway?"

As soon as I spoke, I regretted my words. I was the expert. I was supposed to be determining what it was she wanted. But my masculinity had been destroyed. I lost my erection. Sweat dripped from me as I dropped to the bed beside her. Here I had been giving my all, and it wasn't enough.

For a moment, I felt like crying. I had been expecting to give her the experience of her life, but it was I who had been blown out of the water. I could hear her sobbing beside me. I began deep breathing to regain my composure.

When I had once more donned my professional hat, I raised up on one elbow. "Can we talk about it?"

She nodded. I learned then that I wasn't the first man who had tried to fulfill her fantasy. But neither was I the first to fail. She had even gone to a swinging party with high expectations only to leave in abject frustration. What happened to the men who had tried and not succeeded, I could well imagine.

When we returned to the therapist, we had grist for many more sessions of therapy. Cora now knew that she was causing her own problem. She had always put the entire responsibility for her orgasms on her partners. Now she finally realized that she could not depend on anyone else to give her orgasms. She had to create them for herself.

But she had been unable to be that assertive, in spite of appearances. She felt guilty and worthless as a sexual being. She was a "ball-buster" through no intention of her own.

My input to the therapist was invaluable. I was able to relate my own frustrations and to empathize with her partners. I had been given permission to do anything and everything I knew how to do, yet nothing I did was enough. I felt helpless and impotent—as any man would under such circumstances.

Cora had fallen into a vicious performance cycle. The harder she tried, the less she succeeded—and the more she blamed her partners for her failures. All the hate and anxiety and hostility she felt against herself came out in this sexual failure. What she really wanted was a mind-blowing experience that would free her from her negative feelings about herself. But sex could never perform that function.

It took months of therapy to help her. When she learned that the less she tried, the greater her pleasure, she was on the way to emotional satisfaction. She even learned to recognize that sexual marathons might have their place as occasional diversions but that genuine pleasure could only be gained from real intimacy and closeness.

I was gratified to be a part of her enlightenment. But to this day I will never forget the lesson I learned myself. I know now that when one just performs, even giving one's all is not enough.

Earlier, in the course of my training, I had learned another important lesson, also having to do with my potency. I was in a sexual enrichment class of both men and women, some of us hoping to go on with surrogate training. At one point we were divided into pairs and sent to separate rooms to perform sensate-focused genital caressing. The purpose of the exercise was to learn as much as we could about our partner's body. This was not to be primarily a sexual experience, but one of sensuality, loving, and caring.

My partner was a female I'd been eyeing throughout the class. We'd talked a bit, and I'll admit my motives in choosing her were not totally pure. I believe I harbored some hope that we'd forget the instructions and just follow our libidos. In fact, I was a bit fearful as to how I'd explain this exercise to my wife when I got home; I was so certain that we'd share more than just a few focused caresses.

We had specific instructions as to what we were to do. The giver was to sit on the bed, back supported comfortably with pillows, legs stretched out and spread. The receiver was to lie down, head at the foot of the bed, with pelvis facing the giver, legs spread and bent slightly, resting on the giver's legs.

My partner chose to receive first. I began to caress her, reminding myself that this was to be sensual but not sexual. I knew I wasn't to worry about her feelings but only to enjoy what I was doing. Actually, I was apprehensive that I wouldn't be able to make it through the exercise without getting an erection, and since I hadn't said anything to my partner, I was uneasy about how she'd react.

I spread body oil on my hands and began to caress her belly, thighs, and vulva. We both closed our eyes. In what seemed like ten seconds, there was a knock on the closed door and the instructor called out, "Time to reverse."

Startled, I looked at my watch. Almost a half hour had passed! Here I had actually spent twenty-five minutes caressing this lovely woman in absolute silence. But what upset me was that I'd become so engrossed, I never became aroused. I glanced at my flaccid penis to make sure it was still there. What had happened?

We reversed positions, and now my apprehension increased. Would she be insulted if I got an erection? What would she do about it? I squirmed and changed positions as she caressed me, waiting for the inevitable stirring in my penis. I glanced at my watch again, finding that only ten minutes had passsed. Nothing had happened. I was so preoccupied with my expected erection that I hadn't noticed that I was enjoying her touch.

I waited some more. At last, frustrated with my unresponsiveness, I decided to forget it and enjoy what little I could. I glanced at my partner's face. Her eyes were closed, her mouth slightly open. She seemed to be listening to music that wasn't there. I don't think I'd ever seen a woman look so lovely. Her whole body was relaxed, and her hands felt wonderful as they moved into every nook and cranny of my exposed body.

When the inevitable knock on the door came, I felt like screaming "Go away, we're not ready yet!" But my partner stopped, took my hands, and helped me up. We embraced and headed back to the meeting room. For the next forty-five minutes, we were all to talk about what we had just experienced.

I had nothing to say. Usually loquacious, I sat in silence as my partner spoke of how she felt both as receiver and giver. I grew more apprehensive with each passing minute. When my turn came to speak, I passed. At last, I was the only one who had said nothing. The instructor turned to me. "Isn't there anything you'd like to share?"

It took me some time to muster my courage. "I . . ." I paused. "I didn't have any problems when I came into this course, and I damned well don't want any when I leave. This is the first time in my life I've had a woman stroke my penis and had no response. Hell, I think I'm impotent."

No one spoke. Frustrated, I continued. "What the hell is wrong with me? What am I going to do about it?"

Again, silence. At last, one of the other men spoke. "You know, I had the same experience, but I enjoyed what went on so much, I really don't give a damn. I'm sure your impotence is only temporary."

Four other men chimed in now, admitting that they'd had similar experiences. One or two had been erect for a while, but then had lost the erection as they got into the exercise. None of them had spoken of this experience during the feedback session. Only one man reported something different.

"When we got into the room, she wanted to do me first. That was okay with me. As soon as she touched my cock, I got a tremendous hard-on. I asked her how she felt, and she said that as long as I didn't expect her to do anything about it, she could care less. However, as she continued, I just came. It was totally unexpected, and I felt uneasy. But she just went on with the exercise, stroking and caressing me until the time was up. She didn't even pause. When it was my turn, I was able to enjoy caressing her without feeling a lot of sexual pressure. I really learned tonight what it means to take for yourself and not worry about your partner. It was a mind blower."

Now everyone seemed to open up. The woman who had been with this man explained how she had reacted. At first she was a bit self-conscious. But she just decided to ignore his response and do as she'd been told—enjoy the touching for herself. It was the first time in her life she'd had such an experience. The other men in the group seemed pleased even though they hadn't had erections or orgasms. They enjoyed the opportunity to lie back and be touched without any need to perform. The instructor was delighted with the entire evening. Everyone assured me that I needn't worry. I wasn't impotent. Quite the contrary, they told me, maybe for the first time in my life I'd learned to contain my sexual energy.

I wasn't convinced. I rushed home to check things out, but I received no reassurance. For the next couple of weeks, I was impotent. I told the instructor in no uncertain terms that there had better be some other exercise to correct the situation before the classes ended, or . . . or else. I wasn't sure what the "else" would be, but I hoped the threat would get some action.

At each succeeding class session, I spoke of my predicament. But no one seemed to care. I was advised to stop being so preoccupied with my penis. I was told not to worry. One man even admitted that he was having a similar problem. And, finally, everyone in the class tried to convince us both (and particularly me, since I was most worried) that the condition was only temporary. "It's just a learning experience," one fellow student remarked. "In the long run, what you learn now will be of benefit when you become a surrogate."

Three weeks after my problem began, it was over. My classmates were right. I *had* learned a great deal from the experience. Finally, after years of being at the mercy of my penis, I was beginning to have control over what happened to it. I was becoming the master of my body. And that control helped me gain insights that would otherwise have been closed to me.

It's a common complaint among most of my clients that men don't seem able to give love without sex. The old saying "Women give sex for love; men give love for sex" appears, in general, to be true. A woman seems to feel that if everything else in her life is good, she enjoys and wants sex. A man feels that if his sex is good, he'll find it easy to make everything else good, too. I know now that this is tied to a man's concern for his erections. He expects that any contact he has with a woman he loves should result in an erection. He doesn't dare risk not having that happen. If he can touch or look at a woman without arousal, when he wants it, then maybe something is wrong with him.

After I became a surrogate, I was asked to undergo further training and become a class leader in the Sexual Enrichment Experience (SEE) class I had attended two years earlier. I was flattered at being asked. Since then, in the three years I've spent as co-leader, I've probably learned more about people than I ever have in my surrogate work. Certainly, I've learned a lot about men, since I don't deal directly with them as a surrogate.

For years, I had been intrigued by the process through which strangers become friends. In the SEE class, I see this repeated again and again. We start with ten or twelve strangers who, twelve weeks later, are usually close, intimate friends. If the class has been successful, and even if the graduates do not become qualified surrogates, they will have learned to transfer what they gleaned from the class to family, friends, and associates in other areas of their lives.

At the beginning of each class, everyone is a bit nervous. Some men admit later that they came to the class hoping to find a sex partner. Some of the women admit to being frightened—so scared, in fact, that they can barely talk. Nevertheless, they have the courage to continue. They, too, occasionally hope to find the right partner. But for the majority of them, as with most of the men, the goal is to gain what the title of the class suggests—an enriched sex life.

One evening, several class members were absent, which

threw our gender balance off. Rather than assign exercises that would have to be repeated later, my co-leader and I decided on a new approach. We separated men and women. I took the men into another room. The women remained where they were. The idea was to talk openly, without worry about how we might affect classmates of the opposite sex. There were to be no special guidelines.

We men were unsure how to start. We ordinarily began our sessions, when both men and women were present, with a group embrace. Though some of the men might be hesitant at first, they soon learn that it's okay when everyone's there and doing the same thing. I suggested that we still start the same way—embracing if we wanted to—and then go on to asking each other questions about sex. Unanimously, it was decided that we'd forgo the touching or embracing and get right to the discussion.

Men's talk usually degenerates into "locker room" banter unless they are united for some special purpose, like a business meeting or a hobby. We had that special purpose—to enrich our sex lives—but we found ourselves strangely handicapped in having no women present to serve as catalysts.

Perhaps that's the reason all the questions seemed to be directed at me. What kind of clients did I work with? How did I adjust to someone who was overweight? I answered honestly, wondering all the while how I might get the other men to open up and start relating experiences and answering questions themselves.

When, at last, conversation dragged, I asked them how they felt about touching other men in a nonsexual way. "Okay, I guess," one man responded amid the nods of the others. "Especially in a family group, or among friends. But I don't feel comfortable with it, and I think it looks silly when men touch each other too much. I always wonder about them a bit."

His response seemed conclusive, but it opened the door to other remarks. The conversation wandered from early sex experiences to feelings about the women in the class, to wives and lovers, to current sexual adventures, to conquests, and, finally, to problems.

"I've always been too shy." The man who spoke had been quiet up to this time. "I have trouble getting sex partners. I wonder, do any of you have any suggestions?"

I was startled. Of all the members of the group, this man seemed the most handsome, gentle, kind, and understanding. I was sure my belief that he was a great lover was shared by all the others. But he didn't see himself that way. He felt weak, indecisive, and unsure of his sexual prowess. As he talked, I realized that, because of problems during his formative years and a bad marriage, he was afraid to take any risks.

The ice was broken. After the class had offered a few suggestions to this troubled man, another began. "Once, when I was a kid, I had an experience I'll never forget. I was with this girl who really knew how to give head. It was great. But, you know, I think it spoiled me. I love a good blow job. But if I feel the gal is only doing it as a favor, it just isn't any good. I want a woman to do it because she likes it. If I have to ask for it, it's never the same."

"Yeah." Another man seemed to come to life. "I know what you mean. I love to give head to a woman. I really do. But if she asks me, I feel as if I'm performing, and it just isn't the same."

A man who had not spoken before cleared his throat. "I've always been in a position of power, particularly over women. My wife never questioned my authority. My daughters were taught to obey their dad. And I have mostly women employees. Now, don't get me wrong. I'm careful not to abuse my position. But somehow I feel very isolated."

We were all interested now. He continued after a moment of silence. "I've always had good relationships with men, but I don't have any close friends. I've never really felt close to anyone except my wife. Even my daughters, whom I love, aren't physically close. I was never even close to my parents. I guess that's why I took this class. I felt a need to touch and be close. And now, after the few sessions we've had, I realize I have a vast need for intimacy. Funny, I didn't even know what that word meant until recently."

Again, he paused. No one interrupted. "My personal secretary has always seemed like a warm, caring woman with the other people in the office and with my family, but never with me. One day, since this class began, I was having a particularly difficult time and felt very lonely. She came in to take dictation and handed me a letter. I touched her arm and thanked her. She looked at me in surprise and left.

"Later, one of the women in the office asked for time off. I have always granted it when possible, but this time, as she thanked me, I gently held her shoulders and told her to have a good day. In the week that followed, I touched, in a nonsexual way, as many women as I could. I even gave my wife a big hug when I came home from work.

"You know, things changed. My secretary brought in a rose from her garden and put it on my desk. As she gave it to me, she stroked my cheek and told me I looked well. And last Friday, when I came in, the women were all waiting for me. I'd forgotten it was my birthday, but they had remembered. They had coffee and doughnuts and some small gifts for me. Each one hugged me and some even gave me a kiss. It was all I could do to keep from crying. No one in the office had ever done that for me before."

I could see that he was close to crying now, just remembering. "I'd always felt the world was such a cold place. I guess, like you've been saying, I took a risk to touch someone, and I wasn't rejected. If nothing else comes out of this class for me, that will have changed my life."

We all clapped and congratulated him. Once more the intimacy of the group deepened. Now we talked about giving because you wanted to, of taking for yourself, and how that leads to pleasure for your partner. By the end of the session, we were all feeling very good. We had done no touching, it's true, and there was much we had still not shared, but we all felt closer than we had before. We were among trusted friends, even though a few of the men admitted that they still hesitated to discuss their deepest feelings.

With a feeling of accomplishment, we headed back to the main meeting room. However, as I approached in the lead, my co-leader held up her hand to indicate that they weren't yet ready for us. So we all headed for the kitchen, where we had a coffee break, discussed the weather and sports scores, and indulged in typical "man talk."

Finally, we got the signal. The women were ready for us to return.

We entered a totally quiet room. As I looked about, I saw that many of the women had been crying. Two women were hugging each other as if they dared not let go. Subdued, we settled down in the places we had vacated. Still no one spoke. At last I took charge. "We men feel we had a very good experience. We got to know each other much better than we did before. How about you? Is there anything that went on here that you'd be willing to share?"

Like us, they had begun by talking about the class. They went from there to discussing us, the men with whom they were sharing this new experience. They all wished there were more men out there in the real world who were as comfortable and close as our group had come to be.

Then they began to talk about themselves, their fears, and their lives. The outpouring seemed never to end. They spoke of the men in their lives, of their need for closeness and loving and hugging. When they were told they could touch, they began by holding hands, but that was only the beginning. One woman remarked that she'd always wondered how big breasts felt. Hers were small. A large-breasted woman offered to let her touch hers. Soon they were all feeling one another's bodies.

Eventually, this led to examining vaginas. One woman gave permission for the others to study hers, and soon they were all involved in this intimate examination. As the one-hour session drew to a close, they felt so close they just hugged one another. "We realized how we were all part of a sisterhood. We support and help each other in so many ways," one woman explained.

Another chimed in. "This is the first time I've recognized that. I've never felt really comfortable with women before. But all those things they say about women being catty and envious aren't true. At least not when we get a chance to know each other."

We've repeated this kind of session many times since that night, and the results are generally the same. In one hour the women develop a bond. They feel a kinship that does not fade and that seems to expand to include all women. The men, even when they feel close and comfortable during the session, do not come away feeling like brothers. There is no touching, no intimacy except on the verbal level. We certainly feel closer after one of these sessions, and we usually learn a lot, but we are so conditioned to behave "like men" that it would take months of such meetings before we might become as vulnerable and close and loving as the women end up being.

One other interesting point. After each of the sessions, I notice a significant difference in behavior between the men and the women. When they rejoin the group, the men seem eager to share their experience with the women. They seem able to be more vulnerable in the presence of women than when they are alone together.

But the women are far more reserved when the men return to the room. They seem to want to hide their vulnerability when men are near. I don't know why, though I have some theories. Maybe, if the sex barriers are broken down and sex role-playing is overcome, men and women can all learn to relate as these women in class do—openly, honestly, and with a confidence that they will not be ridiculed. And then we may all be able to enjoy the wonders of true intimacy.

8

JUST WHAT *DO* YOU DO?
Pathways to Developing Intimacy

I've said a lot already about what we surrogates do when we work with a client. Whether we're male or female, or working with a straight or gay client, we follow much the same routine. We begin with sensate-focus exercises. While establishing a rapport, during which we learn all we can through talking, we continue on a rather standard set of activities, each organized to allow us to get closer to our client's real needs. Only after seven or eight weeks of such increasing intimacy are we in a position to ferret out specific problems and to tailor the therapy to fit the individual with whom we are dealing.

The surrogate's role is multiple. We act as teachers, investigators, and lovers. This means that, for the period of contact, we must feel a strong attachment to our client. I have often come to admire and respect my clients. I even fall in love with them. But this love is transitory, lasting only for the period of our work together. We both know we'll be together for a period of just ten to twenty weeks, and so, from the beginning, we are prepared for separation.

Because I have truly learned to take what I need from each relationship, I am constantly growing. My investment of energy in my clients' lives yields a high return. For every unit of energy I put into these temporary affiliations, I am paid back at least tenfold. I should be that lucky with the stock market!

One other matter needs to be considered. Why is it okay for a surrogate to have sex with a client while a therapist definitely should not? Members of the therapeutic community generally agree that the worst thing that can happen to a client is to become intimate with the therapist. This applies whatever the sex of client and therapist, though it is most often a problem when the therapist is a man and the client a woman.

There are reasons for this taboo. The client-therapist relationship is very delicate and has many components. The therapist has tremendous power over his client, much like the power of a father over a very young child. He knows all her deepest secrets. She trusts him implicitly, and she often falls in love with him. But it is the love of a child for a father, or a pupil for a teacher. Knowing he is unattainable builds the relationship, which is further strengthened by the development of respect and admiration. The therapist becomes a support for his client. She knows she can turn to him for counseling and emotional guidance. If he then tells her that he has the magic penis that will solve her sexual problems, he is destroying everything they have built together. For there will come a time when he will abandon her, when he will have to move on to new clients. At that time, because of the intimacy of their relationship, she will feel rejected. Her trust will have been violated.

Then she will remember that she paid for those sessions which her therapist used for his gratification, and she will feel used as she may never have felt used before.

Even though the client may have been the one who initially asked for sex, the damage will be the same. However, there may be times when it's appropriate for the therapist to suggest that the client would benefit from a sexual experience.

When a surrogate is brought in, the dynamics of the situation change. Most important, the therapist serves as a supervisor of all that transpires. The confusion a client may feel if sex surrogate and therapist are combined in one person is eliminated. The therapist's role is now clearly defined as someone with whom she can talk about her insights but who remains out of the sexual part of her treatment. If she feels that the surrogate has used her, she has some recourse. The therapist can explain what has happened or even opt to dismiss the surrogate and find someone else to take his place.

The therapist remains objective and thus better able to determine what the problems are. It is the therapist who may suggest the help of a surrogate in therapy, and if the client declines to accept this suggestion, the relationship with the therapist is not damaged. Even if the surrogate must leave, the client never feels abandoned. The therapist will stay until the client is ready to move on.

In a sense, we surrogates are extensions of the therapists. We can do what they must not. They will deal with us if a relationship gets out of control. If we push too hard or behave in an unsatisfactory manner, a client can go to the therapist and have the situation analyzed objectively. Often, emotions that clients keep hidden—emotions that might not ever be discovered in talk therapy or in an intimate relationship between therapist and client—become visible because of the surrogate's presence.

I happen to find it easier to work with female therapists. I believe this is partly because a client feels that she has alternatives, like a child who goes to Mother when

Father disappoints her or refuses what she asks. When I work with a male therapist, I'm aware that he and I must be careful to avoid giving our client the feeling that we're ganging up on her. We also have to be careful so she doesn't feel we are conspiring to give me pleasure, or that the therapist is probing into what happens between his client and the surrogate to satisfy his own prurient interests.

We surrogates work with clients in a variety of ways. They run the gamut from closely supervised to almost totally independent. In a closely supervised modality, we have our meetings while the therapist is nearby at all times, literally available on call, such as when I meet a client at the Center. Generally, in that situation, I meet with the client and the therapist together for about twenty minutes. Then the client and I go to a separate room in the building, where we carry out our exercises. We work for about forty minutes and then return to the therapist's office for discussion about what took place and to make plans for our next meeting.

At the opposite end of the spectrum are meetings that take place either in my home or the client's. In such cases, I may get a phone call from a therapist who asks me if I have time to work with a client. If I say yes, I will be told that the woman will call me to arrange a time. Generally, in this situation, the three of us will meet in the therapist's office for an introduction and discussion. Subsequently, all our meetings will be away from direct supervision.

Generally, the client will come to my house. However, if she has no convenient form of transportation, I may agree to make house calls and come to her. In very rare instances, we may go to a motel. This has many disadvantages. First, it is costly, and the client must pay for the workspace. Second, it is very easy with such meetings to get the feeling that we are getting together for an affair—not for therapy. Such a situation may become demeaning to the client, making it difficult for us to achieve intimacy.

I am most comfortable and my clients feel most accepting when, after the first meeting with the therapist, my new client and I continue our meetings at my home. There, we can relax, have a cup of coffee or a glass of wine, and feel under no time restraints. I contact the therapist either just before or just after each session to discuss the case. The therapist continues to see the client weekly, as do I, and we compare notes. Because we are in regular contact, I can tailor my work to augment that of the therapist.

At the first session I spend with each client, we are both somewhat anxious. I wonder what she thinks of me, and I'm concerned as to how I will be able to help her. She, too, is worried about my reaction to her. Often, she may feel uneasy about paying for what she perceives as a sex partner, since she still doesn't know what will happen between us.

The first thing I do is establish a way of greeting—something that will be ours for the duration of the relationship. Usually it's a hug, or something that encourages nonthreatening physical contact. We move from hugging to nonsexual caressing of those parts of the body that can be reached without disrobing. These are the sensate-focused caresses that are so valuable in helping a client learn to take enjoyment from touching. We caress each other's hands. We stroke and feel each other's faces. The emphasis on these simple acts is the same as that put on body massaging, which might come later. I am to caress my partner for my own pleasure. I am to think about how I feel while I'm touching her. When she begins to stroke my hands or my face, she is to keep the same focus. She is not to think about how I am reacting, but rather about her own enjoyment.

This is very critical, especially with women. Far too many women are conditioned to think only about others. They grow up doing things to please their fathers. When they mature, they may have sex with a boyfriend—often only because he wants it. When they marry, they continue the pattern. They may even be so centered on their partner's reactions that they aren't aware of their own feelings. This simple, nonsexual exercise begins their exploration of their own responses and emotions.

Two examples illustrate how varied first sessions can be. Julia and Gloria were both mature women, but there the similarity ended.

When I arrived at the therapist's office to meet Julia, she was not present. The therapist asked me to sit and began her explanation. "I want you to understand Julia before you meet her. She appears to be outgoing and effusive, but inside she's very tense. She's never had contact with any man other than her ex-husband. When you're alone with her this first time, I want you to be particularly careful. Don't touch her or be forward in any way. She needs help badly, but she's so apprehensive that she might be frightened away if you move too fast. Don't even try the hand caress unless you're sure she's ready for it."

Julia was a large woman, somewhat older than my average client, and she did seem to have a very outgoing personality. The three of us talked for a while, and then we were directed to go into another room to get acquainted.

As we closed the door behind us, I realized a lot rested on what I did in the next few minutes.

"Shall we sit down?" I moved toward a chair, trying to ignore the bed that occupied one wall of the room.

Julia hesitated only a moment. "Aren't we supposed to hug?"

Surprised, I nodded. "We don't have to. I don't like there to be too many 'supposed to's.' We can just talk and get to know each other better."

"I think we ought to hug."

I held out my arms. I certainly wasn't here to argue with anyone.

Julia stepped into my arms and pressed herself against me. I could feel the tension in her body, so I released her, remembering the therapist's words of caution.

Then she began frantically removing her blouse. As I stared, she let it fall to the floor and immediately grappled with the buttons on my shirt. Was this the woman I had been told to handle with kid gloves? I'd always felt this particular therapist was unusually insightful, but now I wondered.

She unbuckled my belt and reached for my zipper as her slacks dropped to the floor. She said nothing, but her actions clearly indicated a sexual energy and arousal that belied the therapist's concern.

Surprised by her unexpected behavior, I pulled back.

She stopped. In tears, she walked over to the bed and sat down. "My God, what must you think of me! I'm so ashamed!" Her words were muffled by her sobs.

I put my arms around her. "It's all right. I understand. I wish I could have done what you wanted. But it wouldn't have been appropriate for you at this time. You'd have felt angry at yourself—and at me, afterward. And then I couldn't have helped you at all." I felt her shoulders relax just a little. "This is important, you know. You should tell the therapist what happened."

She shuddered. "I couldn't. I'm so ashamed."

It took some persuasion, but I finally convinced her that I should go down the hall and get the therapist. This

was a perfect example of the value of having the therapist nearby when I work with a client. Had Julia been a different kind of person and had we been alone, I might have been accused of rape.

When I told the therapist what had happened, at first she didn't believe me. But she came with me, and after a three-way conversation that lasted about a half hour, she left. Julia and I were once more alone, but she was feeling better now, having been reassured by the therapist that what she did was okay under the circumstances. She understood for the first time how her uncontrolled sexual energy was contributing to her unhappiness and tension. We spent the rest of the time touching, embracing, kissing, and, finally, talking some more.

In Julia's case, in order to get her sexual energy under control, the therapist suggested that we change the normal routine, spending the first few sessions having sex. For the next three meetings we most certainly did expend sexual energy. I felt like a gourmet who had suddenly entered a banquet hall. Fourteen sessions later, Julia was a changed person. She learned to identify her goals and to ask for what she wanted, both in sex and in other aspects of her life. As often happens, Julia learned that getting a grip on her sex life influenced every part of her existence.

The other first session that was far from normal occurred when I met Gloria, who sat facing me as I entered the room. She was attractive, with fine, diminutive features. She had lovely hands and green eyes, and her thin lips were smiling. Despite this, I had an instant reaction. This was a cold fish.

After a short conversation, the therapist told us to go into another room and do the hand caress. I did Gloria's hands first, taking the usual ten minutes or so. Then we reversed positions and she began to caress one of my hands. She moved awkwardly, in a fumbling manner that was both brusque and uncomfortable for me. She stopped after two minutes or so and looked at me inquiringly.

I felt she wanted to get out and was only staying around because she wondered what foolishness I would suggest next. I began with a question. "How did you feel when I caressed your hands?"

"Okay."

"Can you describe your feelings?"

She was silent for a moment, and then she blurted out, "What do you really think of me? Please, be honest."

I was taken aback. But from years of experience, I know that only if I'm honest can I progress with a client. "You're a very attractive woman. I like your hands. But you come across as being very . . . cold."

"Frigid?"

I ignored the question. "But I feel that under your veneer of disinterest is a very warm, affectionate person trying to get out. Your eyes tell me this." I saw that she wasn't going to speak, so I continued. "I feel as if you're withdrawn because you don't like yourself very much. I feel that you think other people don't like you, either. I felt that you just pretended interest in the hand caress exercise because you're afraid to let your real feelings come out."

It was a long speech, and I was beginning to worry about its effect on her.

Gloria smiled weakly and stood up. "Shall we go back now?"

I followed her back to the therapist's office. She had little to say except to agree that she'd be back next week.

After she left, the therapist and I talked. I told of my one-sided conversation, and we agreed that we'd probably never see Gloria again. My big mouth had chased her away.

But she did return. She told me later that when she drove away that first week, she was determined to forget the whole thing. But she had come to therapy for help, and she was sure that because I was truly candid with her she would get it if she returned. "You're the first man who was really honest with me. I didn't realize that was how I seemed to others."

In the weeks that followed, Gloria learned to trust me enough to allow herself to get turned on, sexually. But if I had given her a "snow job" that first session, I would never again have had the chance to be of help to her.

With most clients, we begin with simple hand touching. Then we move to more intimate touching, but we keep the emphasis on getting pleasure. Our first sensate-focused caressing involving the full body does not include touching the genitals. This is to help the client see that touching does not have to be sexual. Only after she becomes comfortable with taking pleasure in massaging me while ignoring any sexual response I may have do we proceed.

Now we begin direct contact with the genitals in an exercise called "nondemand genital pleasuring." The touching includes looking, stroking, examining, and feeling the genitals of the other person but without the pressure of being obligated for the other person's pleasure. For many women, this is the first and only time in their lives they've been able to examine male genitalia in a nonthreatening, nonperforming, and "safe" manner. Similarly, when I am the giver and I'm stroking her genitals, it's important that the client take her pleasure and not be concerned with my arousal or what to do about it. Usually, by this time, she recognizes that we are both enjoying what is happening, and she is beginning to feel more at ease.

At any point along the way, if the therapist and client

both feel it necessary, the work with the surrogate can be terminated, although it will ordinarily continue for many more sessions.

The next step is the sexological examination. In this we exchange active and passive roles again, as we did with the genital caress. It's rather like "I'll show you mine if you show me yours." I try to emphasize that the sexological is not a pelvic exam, since most women have had such bad and sometimes painful experiences associated with this procedure. Instead, the client holds a hand mirror and, perhaps for the first time, examines her own genital area in detail. We talk about all the features that are visible—the clitoris, the labia, the pubic hair, the size and shape and color of various parts, and how she looks to herself.

Following this, we insert a speculum and she sees her vagina and cervix. Then, with her permission, I withdraw the speculum and insert a finger so that we can find out how different areas of her vagina feel to my stimulation. Again, this is not done for arousal purposes, but if she does get aroused, it's all right. This is an educational procedure which most women find enlightening. Included in the process is a lecture on the similarities between men and women, and all of her questions are answered. Although most clients are apprehensive when this exercise begins, by the time we're through they feel relaxed, comfortable, and informed.

Then it's my turn. I lie down on the bed or table and spread my legs. If there's one around, we use a gynecological table with the stirrups for the feet. As I've mentioned, such a table makes me aware of how exposed a woman is when she faces this particular examination.

As my client looks at and touches each part of my genitals, I name it and tell her its function. I have gone through this often enough so I usually do not become aroused, but if I do, I reassure her and tell her to proceed. It's my erection and I'll be responsible for it. She is not expected to change procedures just because of something I did.

Sometimes, this sexological examination is preceded by a viewing of our bodies, usually as we stand together facing a mirror. We look at and discuss every part of each body, remarking on both dissimilarities and likenesses. We note scars and hair and also consider how we feel about ourselves. This is important, because it brings to the forefront a client's self-image. I've had clients with lovely bodies who looked on themselves as ugly. And I've had clients who were so obsessed with scars that they couldn't see their bodies at all. But all clients seem to react well to this mirror exercise, for they dare at last to speak of the imperfections they abhor. And they often come to realize that, at least in the eyes of another observer, they have no reason to be ashamed.

As the sessions continue, I am able to discover what specific problems trouble a client. Women really don't pay me to have sex with them. They pay me to become their temporary partner, their teacher, someone to take the time to share their most intimate thoughts. I never truly have the role of lover, even when we do have sex, for I must always be aware of what my client is doing and feeling. In the process I serve as a bridge, transmitting any insights I have that might throw light on the problems that brought my client to a sex therapist.

I serve one more important function. At the beginning of our time together, I impress upon my client that ours is a temporary relationship that will come to an end. So, from the start, we prepare for termination. This, I feel, is crucial to the client's development.

I begin by being in control. I tell her what we're going to do, while at the same time assuring her that I'll never force her to violate her own limits. As we progress, I insist that control is gradually turned over to her. Eventually, this will enable her to make the correct decision as to when we should terminate our relationship.

When this decision by the client is reached, we have a closing session in which we discuss what we've each learned, taking care to settle any unresolved conflicts before we part. Because of this procedure, every client learns more than just sex skills. She learns to accept the inevitability of parting that is inherent in every relationship. And she learns to accept responsibility, not only for her own emotions but for how she chooses to express them with a partner of her choice.

One thing I never do is offer or promise to make everything right for a client. No surrogate ever will. What I do is listen to her problems, offer to help her work them out, and, with the aid of the therapist, present her with options that can usually make things right for her. I show her how she can help herself, how she can take responsibility for her emotions and her life. And I show her that by doing so she is only becoming responsible for herself—not behaving selfishly. And sometimes I don't have sex with a client at all. Her need may be for intimacy, not a good screwing.

In this, we surrogates differ from the prostitutes we are occasionally accused of being. A prostitute may give her client the sex he demands, but she doesn't deal with the inner disturbances that cause him to seek sex for hire. It may be fun, but it isn't therapy.

The fact is that both men and women reveal themselves most clearly in periods of intimacy. Many times, in the midst of sex, some little word or act will expose a problem that has remained hidden during talk therapy. It's the task of the surrogate to remain alert to these little cues and to bring them to the attention of the therapist. This doesn't mean I violate the client's trust. I've often been asked not to tell anyone, including the therapist, what happened during a sex session. I have always given that promise—and kept it. But, at the same time, I have urged my clients to discuss it with the therapist themselves. Fortunately, I've been successful in my attempts at persuasion. Insights that are ignored can't be brought to bear on problems.

Often, a male client will ask a female surrogate to perform fellatio on him. This happens if he feels it is her duty and the reason that he is working with her. At such times, the surrogate politely declines, as I did when Julia wanted intercourse, explaining that this isn't her reason for being there. Surrogates do not take their direction from a client but from the therapist. Our duty is to delve into the motives behind a client's requests and demands and convey our insights to the therapist with whom he or she is working.

Most surrogates teach social as well as sexual skills. We help clients who have never dated learn to ask for dates and how to behave when they are accepted.

One female surrogate friend told me of working with a nineteen-year-old young man who was brought to her by his parents. Because he'd have nothing to do with girls, they thought he was gay. She found that he was simply unsure of his sexual orientation—or of anything else about himself. She began the therapy by taking him to museums, to the beach, to libraries. They had long conversations. And they role-played situations where he might meet other people. Only after some weeks did they progress to sexual skills. He learned then that he wasn't gay, nor had he ever been. He had just been too shy and socially ignorant to get close to anyone.

We deal with many kinds of problems. The most common ones that female surrogates encounter are impotence and premature ejaculation. I generally work with women who cannot have orgasms or who have great difficulty reaching orgasm. Both male and female surrogates deal with painful intercourse, lack of sexual desire, and the special problems of the handicapped.

We work to improve a client's self-image and to foster assertiveness in both sexual and nonsexual areas. We teach the skills necessary to initiate and terminate relationships. My sessions with any one client are usually two hours long and may continue for periods as short as five weeks to as much as a year. Even though we close at the end of the period of treatment, we must be available to the client if further help is needed. However, a request for further contact must come through the therapist.

Occasionally, I may have what we term an "intensive" relationship with a client. I may spend ten to twelve days in almost constant contact with her. This happens if the client is from out of town and has limited time available. In such cases, I work for a preestablished fee. I may be with the client almost continually, during which time the therapy is intense and specific. This arrangement is an emotional drain on all concerned—therapist, client, and surrogate—but it is a very effective means of treatment.

I am often asked if I worry about venereal disease. Of course I do. But I also take precautions to prevent any problems. Every time I'm paired with a new client, I go to my doctor for a complete checkup. I offer to show clients the results of the test so they can feel confident that I am not infected. I also let them know that if intercourse takes place, I will wear a condom if they wish me to. This usually sets any possible worries to rest.

As for my getting any diseases from them, I consider it highly improbable, since they are not generally sexually active. I can truly say that in all the years I have been a surrogate, I have neither given nor received any venereal disease. I do not have to be concerned with contraception, since I had a vasectomy many years ago. However, one client refused to believe me, so I had a sperm count taken to reassure her.

I'm sometimes asked if there is such a thing as a typical client. The answer is no. I have dealt only with heterosexual females, but there are surrogates who work exclusively with homosexuals, and surrogates who are bisexual. What's more, there is no one kind of person who makes a good surrogate. However, there is a need to match a client to a surrogate, just as it is important that the therapist be someone with whom the client can relate.

What I feel is important about the surrogate-client relationship is that it is set up as an affiliation that must end—albeit gently. The client participates as much as the surrogate in the changes that take place. The goal is to teach the client that although sex with a partner is very pleasurable, he or she does not have to rely on that partner for satisfaction.

I believe this can best be taught by a surrogate of the opposite sex. When a female client returns to "real life," she'll be dealing sexually with men. Whatever she learns in a women's consciousness-raising group can fall by the wayside if she has not learned to relate on an equal basis with the men in her life.

The main goal of sex therapists and sex surrogates is to reeducate. Once the problems of our clients are understood, and they know what it is they want, we help them unlearn bad sexual and emotional habits. We help them master the art of asking for what they want without being devastated if they don't get it. We role-play with our clients, as I did with Angie, to give them positive new behavior patterns that will help them as they adjust to a life in which they dare to be sensuous and sexy.

In the end, it is the woman who heals herself. It is she

who finally sees the causes of her problems and directs her energies to change. If I, as her co-partner in this adventure into self-understanding, considered her to be less capable of growth than I was, I would stand in her way, even though I might not know it. And any surrogate who did that would not continue long in the field.

9

THE G-SPOT
The Excitement of Giving Pleasure

One major impediment to intimacy between men and women is the speed with which many men become aroused and reach orgasm as opposed to the slower, more leisurely lovemaking women need if they are to have a similar experience. There's much evidence that this is a prevailing cause for sexual imbalance in a relationship.

In attempting to explain this disparity, some people attribute it to a man's having a larger number of highly sensitive arousal spots in the genital area—such as the entire head of the penis, or the point just behind the head which, if stroked, often brings about quick orgasm. Generally, it is assumed that a woman's equivalent sensitive area is located only in the small head of the clitoris and that no other spot brings about the same kind of arousal.

My experience has indicated otherwise, and in the last few years research has confirmed my own observations. In 1981, I found the following three articles in the *Journal of Sex Research*, Vol. 17, No. 1 (February 1981), the publication of the Society for the Scientific Study of Sex, of which I am a member: "Orgasmic Expulsions of

127

Women: A Review and Heuristic Inquiry," by Edwin G. Belzer, Jr.; "Female Ejaculation: A Case Study," by Frank Addiego, Edwin G. Belzer, Jr., Jill Comolli, William Moger, John S. Perry, and Beverly Whipple; and "Pelvic Muscle Strength of Female Ejaculators: Evidence in Support of a New Theory of Orgasm," by John D. Perry and Beverly Whipple.

As I read the articles, my mind raced. For years, I'd been hearing about women who discharged liquid during orgasm. I'd even encountered a few myself who would get so aroused while having an orgasm that they would actually ejaculate liquid. I'd never known why this happened to some women and not to others, and I had no real explanation for it happening at all. Here, for the first time, was some legitimate inquiry into the matter made by a reputable group of scientists.

This was my first acquaintance with what is now known as the *Grafenberg spot*—the G-spot. The name was new, derived from Dr. Ernst Grafenberg, who wrote about the spot in the 1950s, but its location, in the vagina, was already known to me. I had worked with women who called it their "sweet spot" because it gave them so much pleasure when it was touched. I was eager to discuss these articles with one of the authors and to compare my private observations with the results of her more scientific study.

Imagine my delight when, a short time later, I had the opportunity to meet Beverly Whipple. I was immediately impressed with her sincerity and dedication to her work. She informed me she was eager to help those thousands of women who ejaculate to know, at last, that they weren't abnormal, for she had found that her subjects were often convinced something was wrong with them. While she made it clear that, by disseminating information about the Grafenberg spot, she was not interested in confronting women with yet another goal to be achieved, she felt certain that if more women knew of their G-spots, it would help them to accept their sexuality and get more pleasure from it. However, she expressed a concern about current research and the logistical problems with getting volunteers and gathering data. Often, when a woman and her lover are used as subject and investigator, the reports are not reliable, and if the researcher is a gynecologist, the volunteers are usually tested in a very clinical environment, which makes intimacy difficult.

But those weren't the only stumbling blocks. There was also the problem that might arise if a physician aroused his client—even for research purposes. It posed a delicate ethical question with which they did not want to deal.

When Ms. Whipple learned that I was a surrogate, she asked if I would be able to furnish her with data which could be accumulated as I worked with my clients. I assured her that this was quite possible. We then agreed that I'd attend one of her workshops to learn as much as I could about the Grafenberg spot. Our affiliation would be unofficial, but because I had access to many women who might volunteer and I was knowledgeable on the subject of sex, Ms. Whipple felt that I could be helpful to her research. I realized that in my constant efforts to show my clients how they could achieve more pleasure in sex, a better understanding of the G-spot would be invaluable. So an arrangement was worked out which we felt would be mutually beneficial.

As a result of that conversation with Ms. Whipple, I discussed the G-spot at a surrogate workshop. One of the women in the class had been a volunteer for an experiment on the subject, and she told me what had occurred. She also helped me locate the spot and gave me guidelines for finding it in other women.

Once I was confident that I knew where the spot was, I

began to ask my clients if I could stimulate them in a particular place and have them tell me how it felt. They all agreed, and their responses pretty much followed the same pattern. First, they had a strong need to urinate, which abated in about fifteen to thirty seconds. Then they experienced an intense sensation within the vagina. As I persisted in stimulating the G-spot, the "intense sensation" usually became very pleasurable.

The second client with whom I tried this had an immediate orgasm. Since she had been inorgasmic when she came into therapy, I knew we had discovered something significant. She told me she'd had that spot touched once before, by a lover. It had been pleasurable then, too, though she hadn't known what it was and neither had he.

The next client was an older woman who was also inorgasmic. When I first touched her G-spot, she reported that she felt nothing special. As I continued, however, it began to swell. I knew she was becoming aroused. As I continued my manipulations, she announced that now it did feel good. I asked permission to continue a bit longer, but she reported that the area was becoming painful, so we stopped. The next time we were together, I asked if I could try again, and she agreed. This time, after a rather lengthy period, she admitted, "It still hurts, but it kinda hurts good."

We continued trying this for the next three sessions, and each time she reported that the pain was less and the pleasure greater. During the fifth session she had an orgasm and a slight discharge. She described the orgasm as "vaginal, deep, and fulfilling." She added that she'd only experienced a similar reaction once before—years ago with her husband, when they were very much in love and had spent an entire day enjoying sex. In fact, she'd had very few orgasms since then, which was why she was in therapy.

In the months that followed, I began working with women who volunteered for G-spot experiments. I encountered women who had orgasms almost as soon as I contacted the spot, and some who felt a little pain at first, but who, when we "worked it out" over a number of sessions, began to enjoy the touch. I concluded that if the G-spot had not been contacted for some time, it usually needed "working out," the repeated stimulation seeming to bring it back to life.

I contacted the G-spot in each of these women and observed their reactions. I did not otherwise become sexually involved with any of them. Often, I wrote my observations down after the fact, relying on my memory of the event. I tried to tape a few sessions, but I found this seemed to interfere with the intimacy of the relationship and so I discontinued that practice early in my investigations.

With the very first female volunteer, I established my procedure. After a phone discussion of the project, we met at my home. Introducing myself, I repeated the reason for my research and described what I would be doing. I gave her an article to read, which I subsequently offered to all my subjects. Then I took a short sex history, which we studied together before we began the examination. By that time nearly an hour had passed, and we no longer felt like strangers.

I led her into the bedroom and told her to lie down fully dressed except for her panties. I stepped into the bathroom and scrubbed my hands, making sure she knew what I was doing. Then I sat on the edge of the bed. "Sexual arousal may occur during this examination, but it isn't necessary," I explained. "The G-spot functions differently at different levels of excitement."

She seemed a bit ill at ease, so I continued. "We won't have sex. That's not what we're here for. This is just to be a short intimate moment. I'll do the analysis. All you have to do is let me know what's happening."

She relaxed a bit. I rubbed lubricant on my hands, talking all the while. "Try to relax. I want you to feel at ease. When you're ready, I'll put my finger into your vagina and locate your G-spot. In the meantime, with your permission, I'd like to caress your body so that you feel a little aroused. It makes insertion of a finger easier."

When she told me she was ready for me to find her G-spot, I moved my finger slowly into her vagina. I described what it encountered and asked her to tell me how each different spot felt. When I reached her G-spot, I spoke. "Okay, this is it. How do you feel?"

She described her feelings, I noted them, and the session was over.

I continued this procedure until my fourth subject. This woman had no trouble with any of the preliminaries, but when she went to the bed she lay there for a moment and then spoke. "I feel silly lying here all dressed with my pants off. Can't I just take everything off? I'd feel a lot more relaxed."

I nodded. "It's all right with me."

She undressed and lay down once more. But she still seemed tense. "I'd feel better if you were undressed, too. Besides, if you're naked, I'll know if you get aroused and I can call a halt. Okay?"

I obliged. She didn't sound as if she wanted to seduce me, and I had no intentions of seducing her. However, we spontaneously embraced after I was nude, and then she lay down once more. She smiled. "That's better. Now I don't feel like a guinea pig."

This became the pattern throughout the rest of my research. To my amazement, every woman, for the most part total strangers to me, went through this routine, ending up naked on the bed and feeling safe, comfortable, and very interested in the project. I never violated the trust they put in me. I located their G-spots and then we got dressed. All of them, without exception, admitted the experience was interesting and rewarding. They left with a new insight into the functioning of their bodies.

Each volunteer had told me how she reacted to my touching her G-spot, such as whether she wanted more pressure or whether I should move more slowly. If one became aroused or indicated a wish to have an orgasm, I told her it was all right. A few requested that I stimulate the clitoris, too, and I complied long enough for them to tell me how that feeling differed from the stroking of the G-spot. If any had orgasms, I'd request permission to continue the manual stimulation to see if they could have more. And if they did, I got permission to keep up the stroking to see if they could ejaculate.

I invariably got consent for continued contact, the second half of each session lasting anywhere from fifteen minutes to an hour. When it ended, we would dress, have a cup of coffee or a glass of wine, and discuss what had happened.

I was at first reluctant to include my own observations in the reports of my research. Who was I to decide what was going on in a woman's body? But there were several discrepancies that made me realize my observations had value. A number of women said nothing about, or denied, ejaculating, yet I witnessed the expulsion of fluid. Two women swore they ejaculated, but I observed nothing. One woman had such strong vaginal contractions that she literally expelled my finger. She reported a "sucking sensation" and was certain that she had drawn my finger farther into her body. I was fascinated with the question of female ejaculation and determined to study it further.

Then I got a call from a friend. She had heard about

my research. She was interested in locating her G-spot and in the idea of female ejaculation as well. She'd been a bed wetter as a child and had always been ashamed of that. As she matured, she retained a fear that she'd urinate in bed. This apprehension was reinforced when she was a teenager. While having sex with her boyfriend, she'd had a powerful orgasm, accompanied by a copious discharge of fluid. "It went all over him, me, and the bed," she explained. "I was so embarrassed. He was disgusted. He thought it was urine, and so did I. I decided I'd never let myself get so out of control again."

I hadn't considered that aspect of female ejaculation before. Together, we wondered how many women there might be who, because they misinterpreted their sudden expulsion of liquid as urinating, were holding themselves under strict control, as she was, and thereby suppressing orgasm. She was determined to change. She'd read books that made her question her reactions to that first-time experience. Maybe she wasn't a freak after all.

We tried one session, just to see how her G-spot felt and how she reacted to having it touched. At first she had the familiar feeling of needing to urinate, and she tightened up. I assured her that in spite of this feeling, most women don't urinate and that she should let me continue. She agreed, and I kept up the "flicking" of my finger against the hard button just inside her vagina, above her pelvic bone. She became extremely aroused, but her old feeling of having to repress an orgasm was stronger than her desire to have one. She asked me to stop, explaining that she was sure continued stimulation wouldn't change her reaction. We quit but set up an appointment for the following week.

At our second session, she was quite apprehensive. She was still very worried that she'd "let go" and urinate all over the place. We talked for a while and I tried my best to reassure her, but she insisted that wasn't enough. She'd have to give herself permission, and she didn't know if she could do that.

I smiled. "So let's pile towels on the bed. If you let go, I'll have something with which to protect myself."

She laughed—and agreed. I stimulated her G-spot, and in a short time she was aroused. I asked her to note any feelings in her body that were different from the way she felt when only her clitoris was stimulated. Even if she couldn't describe the differences, it seemed important to me that she be aware of them.

Her clitoris was already aroused. I stroked it a few times, noting that it was swollen and sensitive. I continued on with her G-spot, asking if she could talk about her responses. She shook her head, so I let her remain silent and simply observed what was happening to her. Within five minutes, she was on the verge of orgasm and announcing that she felt as if she was going to urinate.

I smiled and reached for a towel. "Let it go. I'm ready."

The deluge never came. Instead, she had a strong orgasm, at the same time expelling a small amount of liquid through her urethra. I was very careful to note its origin, because some critics of the G-spot claim that the discharge, if it does occur, is merely lubrication from the vagina. I stayed with her as long as I could, holding my hand so as to retain some of the liquid. Then I moved away.

She still had her eyes closed. "Stop, please. It's too much."

I held up both my hands. "I *have* stopped."

Her eyes shot open and she looked at me. "But I still feel you touching me there."

We examined the fluid she had expelled, and it clearly was not urine. She was delighted. She knew now that, even as a young girl, she had not urinated. It was, as she put it, "neat" to know that she was just ejaculating.

A point to remember: It is important to distinguish between ejaculation and urinary incontinence. Women who suffer from incontinence should consult a gynecologist, since there are many causes of this affliction.

This was the first time, but not the last, I worked with a woman whose G-spot seemed to have a memory. Many times, after this initial experience, I removed my hand only to have a volunteer remark that it still felt as if I was touching her. One woman with whom I worked claimed that she felt the stimulation and a "need to urinate" that lasted all day until she finally masturbated and had an orgasm. This tendency of the G-spot to remember stimulation is fascinating to me, and something that I feel needs further research.

One problem I faced, as far as my investigation was concerned, was the knowledge that sex therapists who discounted the importance (and sometimes even the existence) of the G-spot insisted that anyone doing research on the subject was really stimulating the clitoris, even though indirectly. This isn't surprising. The G-spot is inside the vagina, just "above" the pubic bone. In a way, it can be said to be just behind the clitoris.

When I stimulated the G-spot, I often used two fingers, sometimes directly on it, and sometimes one on each side of the spot, around its periphery. During this time I listened carefully to the subject's description of her feelings. Using the information I had gained during the first session, I tried to concentrate attention on the most sensitive area, which was different with each woman. And all the time I asked for feedback.

More women had orgasms during the second session than the first. I suspect the greater influence of our increased familiarity, because of which no one was now reluctant to have an orgasm or to ejaculate. I had covered the bed with plastic under the sheet, and there were plenty of towels nearby.

I had intended to send any samples I got to a lab for analysis, but the problems of freezing the liquid, storing it, shipping it to the lab, and then waiting for results was just too cumbersome. I finally realized that that part of the research would have to be done in cooperation with a medical facility, and after a grant was obtained which would pay the lab expenses.

At the end of this second session, the volunteer and I again dressed and sat discussing what had happened. I asked a set of questions and requested that the subject rate her orgasm on a scale of one to ten. I always recorded the answers as soon as possible after the subject's departure. I then kept all records, including my own assessment of the strength of each woman's responses. When there was ejaculation, I reported what I saw (specifically, the expulsion of the fluid from the urethra), the condition of the nipples, changes in configuration of the body, and body movements.

One other woman warrants special mention. Kim was in her mid-thirties, divorced, and had had several sex partners since her marriage dissolved. She had just broken up with a lover and explained that she didn't feel very sexual. We agreed that I would just show her where her G-spot was and the session would end.

However, when I touched the spot, she decided she wanted me to stimulate it to see what would happen. After about ten minutes, she announced that she didn't think she could have an orgasm. So we stopped and talked a while. I asked her if she was agreeable to having her clitoris stimulated to see if she reacted differently when it was stroked than when I touched her G-spot. I inquired whether she wanted to do it herself or if I should. She chose to have me do it, so I proceeded.

In about three to five minutes of stimulating her clitoris, she had an orgasm which she rated at about five or six. This, she explained, was about average for her. We dressed, and she agreed to return in three weeks.

At the second session she was more relaxed, though still overwrought because of the breakup of her love affair. She asked me to hold her for a while before we began the session, so we lay together, holding, touching, and caressing in a nonsexual manner. Only when she announced she was ready did I insert my finger and locate her G-spot.

Within two minutes after beginning the stimulation, the G-spot began to swell, which I considered a reliable indication of arousal. Kim said she didn't want to talk anymore—that we could discuss her feelings later. She just wanted me to continue stimulating her G-spot as long as I could. I nodded my assent.

Within another ten minutes, she had an orgasm. I judged it to be rather small, but it definitely was there. Her nipples were erect, her p.c. muscles had contracted, and there was an enlargement and retraction of her clitoris. For the next forty minutes, I continued the stimulation. I was careful not to touch her clitoris as I stroked the G-spot with a slow, steady rhythm. She had about twenty orgasms, coming about two minutes apart.

After each one I asked if she wanted me to stop, but she always replied no. Later, she explained that these orgasms were rated at about seven or eight, and she was hoping for a ten. That did not materialize, however. She finally asked me to stop because her vagina was getting numb, even though she felt she could have come again. My fingers were tired, so I complied. But then I asked if she'd like her clitoris stroked and she agreed. I did it for a while but didn't seem able to hit the right spot, so she took over. Now she had one final orgasm. At last she felt no desire to continue. For the first time in her life she was completely drained.

After we dressed and made some coffee, we discussed what had happened. She felt that each orgasm was different, though she couldn't say exactly how. She summed up the afternoon as "interesting." She told me that when she had sex she always stopped after one orgasm because her partner seemed exhausted. She had always wondered just how far she could go, but she'd never had a man willing to keep the stimulation up as long as she wanted.

She told me that she often didn't experience orgasm during intercourse, and so I suggested that she ask her partner, when she again had one, to stimulate her G-spot manually before intercourse. After she had had an orgasm or two that way, he might insert, letting his penis take the place of his finger. This might condition her to react more strongly to insertion. I have found that this technique allows a woman who has been accustomed to using a vibrator to transfer her reactions to intercourse, and I could see no reason why it wouldn't work from finger to penis as well.

All in all, I spent twenty months examining over two hundred volunteers. My initial motivation was to discover if I might be able to use knowledge of this sensitive area to help my clients. But as my research continued, and I began to give lectures and workshops on the subject, many of the women I met were interested in my research. My list of volunteers expanded.

I held one workshop, primarily for professional therapists, that was specifically designed to help them locate their G-spots. One woman stepped with me into a specially equipped room and said that she just wanted me to touch her G-spot but not to manipulate it at all. I agreed and began the exploration.

When I contacted her G-spot, she jumped. "My God, I've never felt anything like that before!"

I immediately held my finger still. "Shall I take it out?"

She didn't reply, but clamped her legs together, effectively locking my hand in position. She moaned, and my hand was suddenly covered with a stream of ejaculate. She was experiencing an orgasm.

I was startled—but she was totally astonished. "I've never had that happen before." She sat up, her face flushed. "What's odd is that I wasn't even very aroused. If anything, I was apprehensive." She looked at my hand, which I was drying on a towel. "And I've never ejaculated in my life. Are you sure I didn't just urinate?"

There was enough liquid on the bed for us to examine, and we both agreed that it was not urine. It was a thin liquid, more like nonfat milk, with virtually no odor. But it wasn't thick or viscous like male ejaculate, either.

The other women had various responses. Some clearly recognized the feeling and admitted they'd experienced that pleasure before but hadn't known the name of the spot that was touched. Others, whose husbands were present, asked me to help their men locate the spot, so they could touch it again when they were alone. One asked if she and her husband could continue because it felt so good. This delayed my working with anyone else, but it obviously gave them both pleasure.

Often, during these workshops, I've been honored by men who have asked me to help them find their wife's G-spot. I've also been touched by the closeness some people have shared as a result of my work. In one workshop, I was approached by a young couple who asked if there was a private chamber we could use. The young woman wanted me to show her husband where her G-spot was located.

With permission from the other members of the group, we retired to a bedroom that was available. I found the young woman's G-spot and helped her husband find it as well. At that point, she announced that she'd never been so turned on before. "Maybe," I suggested, "I should leave you alone for a while." They agreed, and I returned to the workshop.

In the two hours that followed, I virtually forgot about the two in the bedroom. When the lecture group dispersed, however, the young man and his wife emerged, their faces radiant. "This has been wonderful," she exclaimed. "And I thought we were incompatible."

They went on to tell me that when they arrived at my lecture, they had almost reached the decision to get a divorce. He was a premature ejaculator, and she thought that she was frigid. But now they knew otherwise. They had not had sex for months prior to the workshop. They had agreed to try sex therapy but didn't know where to go. Actually, they had come to my lecture with the hope that I could suggest a therapist for them.

When I left them alone in the bedroom, he continued to play with her G-spot for almost an hour. She had never been so turned on, and he was so involved with her that he wasn't concentrating on his own pleasure, as is common with most premature ejaculators. When they realized this difference in how they were acting from how they had made love before, they spent the next hour enjoying each other. They reported they had the best sex session they'd ever experienced.

I gave them the name of a sex therapist, but so far they have not called her. I think they learned enough about each other that night, and about loving and caring, so they are now able to deal with their problems by themselves.

I find it interesting that the results of my investigations did not always concur with others in the field. Some researchers weren't always able to locate the G-spot on a client, whereas I never found a woman whose spot I couldn't immediately discover. They had very little reportable luck in witnessing ejaculation, while I encountered ejaculation in ten to fifteen percent of the women I worked with. Some investigators came across many women with G-spots too sensitive to be touched, whereas I detected only a few older inorgasmic women who noted pain when I contacted their G-spots, and their reactions usually changed after I worked with them over a period of a few weeks.

All the other researchers carried on their work in clinical settings with a gynecological table. The women were gowned and draped, a surgical glove and lubricant were used, and, usually, at least one witness was present to observe what transpired. For these researchers, the average length of time, from start to completion, of the search for the G-spot was only a couple of minutes. All this was considerably different from the modality I used, both in time involved and intimacy established.

If I learned anything, it was that different women react very differently to contact with the G-spot. A woman who has reached a high level of general sexual arousal, who is at a particular point in her menstrual cycle, and who is freely expressive in her sexual response, reacts far differently than a woman who is inhibited sexually and is in a different phase of her menstrual cycle.

As the possibility of publishing this book became a reality, I gradually reduced and finally quit all research. I continue to instruct couples in the location of the G-spot, but it is to give them a tool for sexual intimacy, not for any research on my part. I feel now that there is enough controversy and interest in the G-spot so that controlled experiments will be carried out by those better qualified to do so.

I do, however, have some reservations. There is a need to determine that fine line between intimacy and an ethical, clinical pursuit of knowledge. I found it difficult to summarize my results because so much occurred in a highly charged emotional atmosphere. Everything I have written down is anecdotal, subjective, and open to criticism. The sessions did not follow a set experimental pattern. I have not been able to subject my data to statistical analysis, and the subjects I used were so diverse that only vague, general conclusions can be reached.

However, I realize that a man and woman in the privacy of their own bedroom might find my results more meaningful. For there they can recreate and intensify, in the intimacy of their own relationship, the results I seemed to get with so many of my subjects. For them, I will state my conclusions, with the clear understanding that I can produce no scientific proof of their validity.

1. There is an area along the front wall of the vagina, up against the pubic bone, that feels different from any other vaginal area, and touching it causes different reactions from touching any other place.

2. This area is present in all the women I have examined, so I therefore assume it should be present in all women. It feels something like a bean or a pea but is a bit more in the shape of an almond. When not aroused, it feels somewhat crinkly and flat, varying in size from that of a dime to a half-dollar.

3. It is in relatively the same place in all women, but the actual depth that a finger must be inserted in order to touch it differs with the size of the woman. In obese women it is embedded in much tissue, and more probing

is needed to locate it. In slim women it is much more frontal and easily felt, since there is less tissue hiding it.

4. With instructions, some women can touch it themselves, but very few can manipulate it because of the angle required.

5. Once the G-spot is found, a woman can direct anyone to its location. However, since pressure must be applied to the G-spot to stimulate it, and many men are not accustomed to doing this, some men still find it hard to locate the exact point. They must turn the hand so that a finger can be bent forward and hooked around the pubic bone before they will be able to touch the spot and apply enough pressure to stimulate a woman.

6. All women report that the first time the spot is stimulated they feel a need to urinate. Since the G-spot is just below the neck of the bladder, this is not surprising. However, after between fifteen seconds and three minutes of stimulation, that feeling generally disappears and is replaced by another. This next response depends on the state of mind of the woman. She might feel arousal or pleasure or pain. The sensation may be unusual, familiar, or wonderful—slight or intense.

7. Though most of my subjects reached a point where they could not stand any more clitoral stimulation, those who derived pleasure from G-spot manipulation indicated they could continue "forever."

8. I found that the amount of stimulation asked for varied with each woman, as did the duration of contact required. And the patterns of arousal differed, too. A woman who took longer to orgasm with other arousal techniques required a greater period of stimulation of the G-spot than did a woman who orgasmed quickly with clitoral manipulation.

9. There seemed to be no relationship between menstrual cycle and response to clitoral stimulation. However,

women who objected to sex during menstruation did respond less to G-spot stimulation during that same period. I do not, however, feel that this is anything more than an extension of their normal uneasiness about sexual contact when they are menstruating.

10. Every woman I stimulated had the same physical response. After a time, the G-spot swelled up. Some women, however, seemed unable to recognize or acknowledge that response. When a woman experienced fatigue or a lessening of arousal, the G-spot grew smaller again.

11. All the women I worked with seemed glad to have had their G-spots identified and located. Whether or not they informed their partner of its whereabouts I don't know. I have not maintained contact with any of the subjects I didn't know before the experiments began.

12. There did seem to be some correlation between the reaction a woman had to stimulation of the G-spot and her age, sexual openness, the position from which the G-spot was manipulated, the strength of the p.c. muscles, and the amount of breast caressing involved. All women reported a pleasurable sensation when there was direct pressure on the spot plus a slow, steady, back-and-forth stroking. Fast, frantic, or erratic stroking seemed far less stimulating.

It is possible to stimulate the G-spot during intercourse. The easiest way is when entry is made from the rear—"doggy fashion." Contact can also be made if the woman is on top, since she can shift her body to bring the head of the penis up against her G-spot. Even the "missionary" position can be modified to allow for this contact. If the woman wraps her legs around her partner's waist while he is on his knees facing her, and then lifts her buttocks up high enough, the head of the penis will encounter the G-spot.

One woman felt threatened when she realized that, by touching her G-spot, I could tell she was aroused before she, herself, was aware of it. But this is not the greatest danger in seeking the G-spot. I have heard several gynecologists tell of women who came in with lacerated uteruses, urethras, and vaginas because they, or someone else, put a foreign body into the vagina while searching for the G-spot. Some have had painful cuts because the finger used had a long nail or because they were subjected to too much pressure or stimulation. Obviously, care should be taken when going on this search. Like the rest of the person, the vagina should always be treated with love and tenderness.

In the popular literature about the G-spot published since 1981, the impression has been given that it's a magic button which, if touched, brings about immediate orgasm. I didn't find this to be generally true, though it did happen occasionally. What I and others seem to be concluding now is that the G-spot is a second gateway to orgasm for women, the clitoris being the first.

Most women report clitoral orgasms as being up front, lighter, although frequently more intense and centered on the clitoris. The vaginal orgasm feels deeper, heavier, fuller, more filling and fulfilling. Women claim that it is more dispersed throughout the uterus, the groin, the breasts, and sometimes the entire body. Some current research, and my own experience, shows that when both areas are stimulated at the same time, the woman feels a blended or combined orgasm. This doesn't occur every time, but it appears to be the most satisfying orgasm of all.

10

COMING BACK TO REALITY
Strength in Self-Acceptance

As a society, we are only beginning to recognize how interrelated all the facets of our lives actually are. Doctors tell us that the food we eat influences our mental capacities as well as our chances of getting cancer or some other terrible disease. We are opposed to mistreatment of children, even in the name of discipline, because we now understand that a child who is treated unkindly may never be able to live a happy life. And this understanding is spreading. We see, now, that every event in our lives influences every other. In the past, we treated our sex lives as separate from our intellectual and business lives. Now we are beginning to see that adult sexual problems may affect both personal and business affairs.

I'm sure that a larger number of people would seek sex therapy if this relationship were more obvious, if a tie between cause and effect were clear and indisputable. But so far, evidence of this relationship is mostly circumstantial. Even when we encounter a sexually frustrated woman who is having difficulties in other aspects of her life as well, few of us recognize a relationship between the two problems.

Yet every once in a while I have a client who proves to me how sexual experiences and attitudes, good or bad, can affect other apparently unrelated phases of life. She may come to the therapist for help in achieving orgasms, for example, but learn far more about herself than she ever anticipated. When her sexual concerns have been cleared up, she'll often find that problems in other troublesome areas of her life have dissipated, too.

Elena was such a person. She had been meeting with her therapist for some time before I was called in. Her acknowledged problem was her inability to have an orgasm, but as I worked with her over the weeks I realized that she was also filled with an inner anger. At what, I did not yet know.

The cause of this anger remained a secret until the afternoon she was late for our appointment. When she did arrive, she was furious. She refused to discuss the reason for her upset, simply announcing that she wanted to go to our room and be held. The therapist agreed. We could forget the structured exercise planned for that session. I followed Elena into the private room reserved for our use.

As we undressed, Elena spoke brusquely. "I just want to be cuddled. If I feel like it later, maybe we can do some general body caressing. But nothing else. Is that clear?"

I recognized the fury in that last question. "Yes." I made sure my voice was free of any tension. "Don't worry. I'll do it your way."

She dropped her hose on top of her other clothing and climbed onto the bed. I folded my trousers and put them over a chair. Then I lay down and slid my arm under her shoulders. I cuddled her beside me, holding her loosely.

She wanted closeness, but I sensed her wish not to be smothered.

And then it happened. Usually, I'm able to control the state of my penis, but this time I failed. Almost as soon as I felt her pressed against me, I got a full erection. Elena didn't notice it at first, but when she let her hand slide down my stomach she suddenly stiffened.

I suspected the cause of her reaction, but I had to be sure. "What's the matter, Elena?"

She mumbled something, pushed me away, and rolled over to face the wall.

I knew she still needed comfort, so I began to stroke her back.

"Don't touch me!" she literally screamed, twisting around enough to slap my hands away.

"Elena, what's the matter?"

Silence.

"If we don't talk about it, you'll be wasting a whole session."

She remained silent. Was she determined not to communicate at all?

Abruptly, she spoke. "You know damned well what's the matter!" She waited for me to respond, but I said nothing and so she continued. "I specifically said I just wanted to lie here quietly and do nothing. I said maybe we'd do a few body caresses. And now you and your damned hard-on are going to want sex."

"What gives you that idea?"

"Don't play games with me, Jerry. What else is a man going to want when he gets a hard-on?" She felt my arm on her hip and pushed me away again. "I really wish I could figure you bastards out. When I want sex, you just aren't turned on. But boy, when you want it, you sure can get hard fast. What's wrong with men, anyway? Can't any of them ever sense what a woman wants?" She turned to

face me but kept her distance. "You're a professional surrogate, but you're like all the others. I'll be damned if I'm
going to pay you after this."

I kept quiet, aware of her need to vent the full force of
her anger.

"Damn you! I should have known better than to get
involved with any man again for any reason. You're all
alike. All you ever think of is your cock." As she spoke,
she began to cry.

I reached out and drew her closer, and this time she
didn't protest. For a while she cried silently. And then she
spoke once more. "I suppose you are different. At least
you didn't try to screw me now."

I grunted my agreement, and she continued. "I guess I
didn't really give you much of a chance, did I? After all, it
isn't your fault that I'm the way I am, or"—she laughed
bitterly—"that you're a man."

"Or that I have a cock that seems to have a mind of its
own," I added.

She laughed again. I was relieved to notice that some of
the bitterness was gone. Cautiously, I joined her.

Our laughter seemed to clear the air a bit, so I began
what has become a rather standard speech for me. "Yes,
I'm a man and, like all other men, I have a penis I can't
always control. But I'm also a trained surrogate and, unlike other men, I feel very strongly that it's *my* penis. I
can, will, and do take full responsibility for it and for its
state, whatever that might be."

I could see the interest in her eyes, and so I went on
with renewed spirit. "What's more, I really enjoy having a
hard-on. It gives me a lot of energy, and it feels good. It
helps me feel sensual and caring and makes me want to
be close to someone. But I can usually control my erections by using my p.c. muscles, by breath control, and by
remembering why I'm with a client. Even when I have an

erection, I don't forget that I'm here for your therapy, not to satisfy myself."

She was beginning to relax, and so was my erection. Once more she cuddled close. When she didn't speak, I continued. "You have to believe me when I say you don't have to do anything about my erection. What's more, you're wrong to judge my state of mind by the condition of my penis. I'm not a sex machine. I can't turn my cock into a dildo, and I can't make it hard or get it soft again on command. But whatever I *can* do with it is *my* choice, not yours. You have no obligation to it at all."

I took a few deep breaths, suddenly aware that I had been talking too fast. We lay for a time in silence.

When Elena began to speak again, she was almost whispering. "I had a fight last night with my boyfriend. It happens all the time, and I just got fed up." She told me, then, how he had awakened her by starting to make love. She realized he was excited, but she wasn't aroused at all. He began to caress and kiss her to get her ready and, in the process, lost his erection.

"It's always the same thing. He wants me *right now,* and when he has to do anything for me, he loses interest." She shook her head. "And besides that, sometimes—right in the middle of sex—he gets soft. He doesn't even have an orgasm, *and he gets soft!* Damn it! I'm tired of men who don't care at all. If he really loved me, he'd be able to stay hard long enough to satisfy me."

"Do you always have sex when he gets hard?"

"Usually. And if I just can't get ready fast enough, I'll suck him off or masturbate him. I know it's hard on a man when he doesn't come if he has an erection. Fred's told me he really gets sore balls. My husband was just like Fred, so I know how men are."

She was silent again for a while. "When we were first married, it was different. I really had orgasms then. But after about six months, we were in a rut. He'd get hard, and I'd have to do something about it, whether I wanted to or not. And by the time I got ready, he was all through."

Our time was almost over. "Let's go back to the therapist." I spoke without moving. I wanted her to be the one to break our embrace. Even though we had only cuddled, I knew she'd feel rejected if I got up first. "I think she ought to know what's happened."

I waited for her response. I knew she remembered my promise that I'd never betray a confidence. She knew I wouldn't repeat what she'd just told me. But I still had the right to urge her to tell it all again—to the therapist.

Elena remained still for a few minutes and then, with a sigh, sat up. "Let's go." She began to dress, shaking out her rumpled clothing. "God, I really was mad, wasn't I?"

I dressed quickly. I could see that discovering the existence of her anger had not freed her from it. That was only the first step. Maybe, in talks with the therapist, she'd get some of that inner rage out where she could deal with it.

The therapist was very pleased with the results of the session that had started with such anger. She recognized that only in such an intimate situation could Elena allow the depths of her fury at herself and others to surface.

In the weeks that followed, her inner rage became the focal point of Elena's therapy. Gradually, she learned much about herself. She saw how she was taking too much responsibility for her partner's pleasure. She understood that it was, after all, what she had been taught to do. When she was married, she fulfilled her wifely duty. In her affairs, after her divorce, she felt obligated to give sexual pleasure to her dates. And now, with a full-time lover, she was still following the same pattern. She was convinced that if she didn't give sex to her men, she'd lose them.

Elena saw at last that she was on a performance kick, and her wish to have orgasms, which had brought her to therapy, was a part of it. She was convinced that men felt put down if their partners weren't orgasmic. She was trying so hard to have an orgasm as a gift for the man she loved that she had no time to enjoy herself.

Once the anger began to dissipate, Elena could accept herself as worthy even if she wasn't giving to someone else. Her entire attitude toward life altered. With the help of the therapist, she began to see how her anger had sealed her away from true happiness, how it had made her feel valueless. In the light of her new knowledge, she began to reevaluate her past experiences.

She recognized that, though some people can perform sexually and not feel the same compulsion in other aspects of their lives, for her, pleasing others had been a full-time occupation. She performed in bed. She performed with her kids. She performed in *all* social situations. She had to be good at everything or she considered herself totally incompetent. And when she didn't meet her own high standards (which was often, since she was only human), she grew anxious and depressed, convinced that she was a failure as a person. Her sexual and social difficulties were inextricably intertwined. That discovery was a major step in reaching a solution to her life's problems.

Now, even though she had decided earlier not to have sex with me, she changed her mind. She told the therapist to inform me so I'd be prepared. And here, contrary to our usual pattern, the therapist and I *did* set things up. It was agreed that I was to pretend I wasn't ready. Elena had to learn that sex was okay if we both wanted it, but that she couldn't get it on demand any more than a man could.

We went off to our room with permission from the therapist to have sex if we both wanted it. But I made no move to begin anything. Frustrated, Elena spent the entire time waiting for me to ask her.

When I didn't, she became angry. "Your cock is hard as a rock." She stared at it as she spoke. "Don't pretend you don't want to have sex with me."

I made no move in her direction. "I do want to have sex with you. But I don't *have* to. I won't die if I don't, and neither will you. I'm not playing hard to get, either. When you want sex, and ask for it, I'll comply if I can."

She stared at me in silence for a while. I felt my erection fading. Besides, the time was up. We dressed and went back to the therapist together. There, Elena explained her frustration and disappointment. "I wasn't brought up to ask for sex. Decent women don't do that."

It was the key the therapist had been looking for. Now the treatment could be completed. In the following sessions, Elena began to examine her life in a new way. She had learned to recognize when she was "performing." Now she faced a new issue. What did she really want—not just in sex, but in every area? How could she get what she wanted if she wasn't willing to face her own reality?

When we met again, Elena understood that in this sexual situation she could learn to do something she had never done before. She could decide what she wanted—and ask for it. While she had the opportunity, she could practice being assertive.

In the next couple of sessions, and with great effort on her part, Elena finally voiced her desires. I tried to comply. When she didn't have an orgasm but I did, she became petulant, although she wasn't sure why. However, her experience with me once more served as grist for discussion with her therapist. There were then more sessions without me in which they probed into the anger she had not yet released.

When we got together again, at the instruction of the therapist, I asked Elena for sex. In a joking manner (at least I *hoped* she was joking), she said no. And then, smiling, she added, "I thought you'd never ask."

This time we enjoyed our hour together. I could sense a change in her. She took responsibility for her own pleasure, deriving some of it from the nice things she did for me. And this time she was not left behind when I had my orgasm. She, too, knew at last how to take pleasure while giving it.

The following week we had our closing session, which we spent hugging and holding but without sex. She continued with the therapist for a couple of months longer, going over each step of her progress and clarifying her reasons for having so much anger and hostility.

The therapy that had started with its focus on a sex problem turned into an examination of her inner anger and how it affected every aspect of her life. When she let go of that suppressed rage, her entire life was altered. She dared, at last, to ask for what she wanted, not only in sex but in her everyday relationships as well. She spoke to her boss and told him what she wanted in her work. To her surprise, she got a new position, a nice raise, and a great deal of respect. Her self-esteem grew. She understood that her inability to orgasm had only been a symptom. The changes within her that had freed her sexually had liberated her social and business life, too. The resentment and anger that had dominated her were gone.

I believe Elena could have reached the same state of understanding and release in "regular" therapy. But I'm certain it would have taken much longer than the six months she spent with me. The intimacy of working with a surrogate opens doors that usually remain closed when a client just sits and talks to a therapist. Maybe it's because when we're nude and touching we dare to be more vulnerable. Maybe it's my willingness to expose my own vulnerability that gives a client courage to face hers. It doesn't really matter what triggers the insights. What's important is that they often serve to shorten therapy.

Shauna was another client whose situation illustrated the pervasiveness of inner anger and the value of using a surrogate as a shortcut to ferreting out the problem. She was in her thirties. Her parents had strict religious beliefs and did not believe in displaying affection. As a child, she had never been beaten or abused in any physical way, but neither had she ever felt she was truly loved.

When she reached puberty, she developed quickly. She hated to wear a bathing suit, because her friends teased her and boys tried to "grab a feel" of her size-36 breasts. In high school she allowed herself to get fat, and that stopped the teasing and grabbing. She was left alone, except for her parents nagging at her to lose weight and to be more friendly.

In her late teens, she decided it was time to change. She went to college, lost weight, and began to work on improving her personality and intellect. But she was still defensive. She replaced her "protective shell" of fat with a rather hard, crude way of behaving. Her self-made aggressiveness came across as arrogance.

Aware that she still had problems, she finally went to group therapy, coming to me later on the advice of her group counselor. At our first scheduled meeting, she burst into the room unexpectedly. "I can use help," she announced, as if she were discussing a car that needed repair. "There are some things in my life that just aren't going well."

She was well dressed and carried a briefcase. As I invited her to take a chair facing the one in which I sat, I had the feeling that she wasn't through with her introduction. I was right. But she put the briefcase down and sat in the chair before continuing. "When I have a problem, I believe in going to an expert for help. But, Christ, I never in my wildest dreams imagined that there was someone around who did what you do."

I explained to her that I usually worked directly with a therapist, but she brushed that aside. "How much do you charge? How long will it take? Exactly what do you do?" She sounded like a business-wise customer set on making the best deal she could.

I decided to counter with questions of my own. "Why did you come to me? How do you think I can help you?"

"I'm a ball-buster." She smiled. "That's how I come on. But I'm really scared stiff. Oh, in business it's okay. I don't take shit from anyone. And I handle people well. But it's a different story when I'm with a guy. I'll tell you, I've tried everything. I had such lousy affairs with men, I went lez. But that wasn't any better. So I'm back to men. But I don't enjoy it. A penis, to me, is just big. Sex hurts like hell when I'm doing it. And in the morning, I hate myself and the guy I've been with."

As she continued speaking, I realized she'd done her homework. She understood that even when she happened to be with a man who was caring and tender, he'd end up hurting her because that was how she set things up. She thought oral sex was disgusting. "Why would a man want to kiss me there? But I'd like to learn to have normal sex without it hurting. Do you think you can help me?"

Tears formed in her eyes. "I've made a commitment to get through this. I'll do whatever you want if you can fix me up. I'll be here when you tell me, but if you're going to start by screwing me, I'm not sure I can take it. Not yet." She dabbed at her eyes with a Kleenex. "However, if that's the only way I can be cured, I guess I can even tolerate that."

I felt a wave of sympathy. Here was a bright, beautiful, articulate woman who was willing to do whatever was necessary to get out of her dilemma. But what a position she was putting me in! If I said the word, she'd undress on the spot and submit to whatever I demanded that she do. I breathed a short thanks for my training. If I took advantage of her now, I could easily ruin her for life.

"I'll see what I can do." I rose to my feet. "Right now, I think all we should do is set up a regular time for our sessions. And maybe figure out a special way of greeting."

She looked frightened. "What do you mean? What kind of special way?"

"How would you feel about a light hug?"

"I don't know. I guess if it's part of my therapy, I could try." She stood up and took a step toward me.

I backed away. "No! I don't ever want you to do something just because I ask you to. If you can't handle a hug, say so."

She seemed startled. Here she was with a man and being told by him that he didn't want her to do what he asked.

"Can you think of anything we can do that wouldn't be threatening to you?"

She shook her head.

"How would you feel if you held your hands out in front of you, like when you used to play patty-cake as a child, and I touched my hands to yours. Would that be okay?"

She smiled. Was she amused at so simplistic a greeting? "Oh, sure. I can handle that." She held out her hands and I touched them lightly. When she left, I wondered if

I would ever be able to break through the barriers that guarded her from unknown hurts.

The next few sessions went slowly. She was apprehensive each time. Touching was difficult for her, and she felt threatened if I approached her. So most of my time was spent proving to her that I meant what I said. If I told her I'd caress her hand, that's all I did. At the end of each of these sessions, she seemed more relaxed, admitting that it wasn't so hard after all. "In fact," she added once, "it was kind of fun."

The first session in which we had a breakthrough began like all the others. She entered, we touched hands, and she met my eyes. "Well, what are we going to do today that I'll be afraid of?"

"We've done sensate-focused caressing of all the parts of the body that are visible. Now I want to do a back caress, and for that we need to undress." I watched her closely. If she agreed, and I felt she did so only to please me, I'd have to back down.

She smiled a wry little smile. "Well, I've been scared every time we've done anything and pleased when we were through. So let's see what happens, okay?"

She reached for her blouse and hesitated. "Are you going to watch me undress?"

I felt a sudden inspiration. "Why don't I undress you?"

She flushed, but agreed. Something in her behavior told me that she was willing to try it more out of curiosity than the wish to please. So I went ahead.

I tried to be smooth and casual, but her necklace caught in her blouse and I couldn't handle it. She laughed and helped me out. Then I reached behind her to unclasp her bra—and the hooks weren't there. She laughed again as she unhooked a clasp between her breasts. "That's great." She sounded livelier than before.

"I'm glad you aren't perfect." She removed her bra and tossed it onto a chair.

I was amazed at the beauty of her breasts, but I said nothing. I didn't want her to think I was complimenting her just to be nice. Besides, what I thought of her breasts wasn't important. It was her own image of herself that had to be considered.

She fumbled as she began to undress me. "I feel so awkward."

"Good. I'm glad you do. When you get over your discomfort with me, you will be able to do this with a real lover, and you'll be okay."

When we were both nude we embraced, but she quickly stepped back. "Oh, oh. I think I'm in trouble." Her exploring fingers had touched my penis, and it was erect. I realized then that like Elena, Shauna believed she was responsible if a man she was with had an erection. "That's how it always begins with me," she continued. "Next you'll be wanting to get your rocks off, and I'll be back in the same old circle I've always been in."

I felt a flutter of excitement. We were touching on a very real problem—her feeling of obligation to men. But there was a difference as long as she was with me. She was convinced that she should let me have "my way," since I was aroused. But, at the same time, she was paying and she wanted her money's worth. She was at an impasse. She didn't want to hurt my feelings, but neither did she want to have this session end as her encounters with men had all ended before.

I knew she wasn't ready to handle this alone, so I stepped back and held her at arm's length. "Look into my eyes and try to see what kind of person I am. I'll do the same with you."

Our eyes met, and we stared at each other for some time. When I saw her eyes falter, I moved on. We studied each part of our bodies in the same way until we reached our groins. Then she smiled. "It's soft!"

"Of course." I went on then with my usual explanation of the difference between an overt sexual situation and what we were doing. I explained that my erection was my problem, not hers. She touched my penis and remarked on how squishy it felt. "Are all men like that when they're not hard?"

When all her questions were answered, we continued with our planned sensate-focused caressing. I was pleased to see that, when she stroked me, she was really enjoying what she did. Already, she was learning to give pleasure by taking it.

When we left, she paused at the door. "Maybe they're not all big and bad and hurtful after all." It was my first of many rewards.

In the next meetings, we continued our sensate-focused caressing and reaffirmed the fact that her goal was important. We were here for her therapy, not just so one or both of us could "get our rocks off." I knew now that I had her confidence. And I knew, too, that nothing could cause me to violate that trust.

The next significant session was the one in which we did the sexological exam. I had advised her to visit a gynecologist to make sure she had no physical problems, and she returned with a clean bill of health. It was my intent to see if her vagina was particularly tight or short, since she had complained of pain during intercourse.

I was glad to see that everything was perfectly normal except for her inner labial lips, which were a bit longer than some. It was possible they might fold in and cause her discomfort. To avoid that, I suggested she apply some lubricant before having intercourse, though she felt no pain when I inserted my finger or the speculum.

After we completed her examination, I hopped on the

table. When we were both finished and dressed, she hugged me. "God, when I think of all the years I suffered because I didn't know this kind of help was available. Thanks." Another reward.

The next session started with a tale of her business. "I lost a big account yesterday. It's the breaks. But, you know, usually I'd have been real depressed. But it doesn't bother me. I know I can go out and get another."

And she did. The next week, she was filled with enthusiasm. "I've started doing things *with* people." She settled on the bed, already nude. I wondered if she realized how far she had already come in being comfortable with herself. "I have lunch with the women at work now, and I'm even accepting a few dates. I'm a regular social butterfly." She leaned forward, her eyes sparkling. "And I've bought a car."

She had already told me that she was afraid to take such a step, so I waited for the explanation. "I talked it over with my accountant. I can manage it, and I really need it. I'm not afraid anymore. And best of all, I met a man."

He was someone at a party she'd attended, and they'd felt a mutual attraction immediately. But though she still hesitated to have sex, she now dared to tell him of her fears. "I figured either he'd understand or he'd just walk away. Whatever happened, it would be easier than having a fight in the bedroom—or disappointing him, like I did so many other men before."

But this man understood. They went to his place and petted and hugged. "I really felt as if I could have raped him. But I didn't. I don't want any more messes. You're going to have to teach me how to do it without it hurting. And I'm scared."

She had no reason to be. Everything went smoothly. She had no pain—no vaginismus. We talked about the arms that got in the way and how to avoid awkwardness. We found what positions were most comfortable for her and what she could do to get him to adjust his speed to suit her. We practiced until she felt she could handle any situation. When she left, I was exhausted, but pleasantly so.

In the weeks that followed she told me about her idyllic weekends. "He's bigger than you. I hope that doesn't hurt your feelings."

I winced. "Of course not."

"But it doesn't hurt. And he's so wonderful and understanding." She lowered her eyes. "He wants to go down on me, and he wants me to do it to him. I want to, too, but I just don't know how. I want to be better than anyone else for him." She didn't have to continue. I was more than willing to teach her.

Our last session was beautiful. We cuddled and held each other and talked. We drank champagne and cried. Shauna's entire life had changed. Her therapist and her group had helped, that I knew, but she was convinced that her association with me had been crucial to her development. She stood up at last, ready to depart. "Will you still be my friend? I'm going to miss our visits. If I need help, can I come back?"

I nodded a heartfelt yes. But I didn't expect to see her again, and I haven't. She had grown past me. She didn't need a teacher anymore. And she certainly didn't need a surrogate. She had a real lover of her own. And, maybe most important of all, she knew how to get what she wanted.

Not all my clients have such spectacular results. Some achieve orgasm, but not much else changes in their lives. I take delight in the fact that most women, when their sexual expression ceases to be a problem, become better, more fully functioning people in all areas of their lives. It's the bonus that more than outweighs the expected value of the therapy.

11

CLOSURES
Healing the Pain of Separation

I once knew an elderly widow who, even though she lived alone, refused to have a pet. I urged her to get a cat or dog. "It would be company for you. Research has proved it's good for people to have pets around."

Her response was revealing. "Oh, no. I don't want a pet. I'd get attached to it, and then, when it died, I'd miss it."

I knew then that she had never properly closed her relationship with her dead husband. I understood her pain. We've all had relationships with others that haunt us—relationships that seem to hang in the air, unresolved. In our daily lives, we're constantly establishing and then breaking off associations with those around us. We don't often realize that every encounter we have, no matter how brief, can affect us.

Perhaps we look forward every day to the arrival of the mailman. Maybe all we say is "good morning," but we're cheered by the brief exchange. Then, one day, someone else delivers the mail. I remember that happening to me. When I asked the new deliverer what had happened to the "old" mailman, she didn't know. "I guess he retired" was all she could tell me. I wonder to this day what happened. Is he well? Did he retire because his feet hurt? It was a relationship I never had a chance to close. I couldn't wish him good luck or thank him for his years of service and his cheerfulness each morning. I couldn't even say a brief farewell.

Suppose a man meets a woman in a social situation and is impressed enough to ask her for her telephone number. If, then, he never phones, she may wonder what she did wrong. Did she offend him? Did she behave in a manner that made him decide she was socially beneath him? She may wonder for some time why he never followed through on their initial attraction.

If a relationship is a long and intimate one, like a marriage or a love affair, or even just long-term dating, the sadness that accompanies its end is greater, and the effect it has on our lives is stronger. If we lose a parent or a sibling, break up with a lover, or get a divorce, we can mourn that loss for the rest of our lives.

Because they carry with them an assortment of incomplete relationships, many people today live with a feeling of emptiness. They have no chance to explain to a friend no longer around the anger they once felt but feel no more, or to tell someone they loved in the past that he or she is still important to them, even though they no longer live together. They exist with many bits and pieces of their lives unresolved just because they never had a chance to say good-bye.

Consider this on a very personal level. Psychologists tell us that unresolved relationships drain strength and energy from our current associations and make us less effective in our day-to-day living. Your brothers and sisters move away and cease to write. Your ex-lover goes on to a new romance. Your ex-spouse now lives in a distant city, married to some new person you've never met. But the strings that once held you to these people may not have been properly cut and tied off. That incomplete portion of your life can keep you from making full use of your present potential.

For most people, intimate relationships that eventually fade may number as many as ten, or perhaps even twenty. But surrogates live through many more. Each client becomes dear to us. We share intimacies and grow close. And then we must go our separate ways. If we were not able to wrap each relationship up and "close it off," we'd be torn apart in time.

I was fortunate in my first experience as a surrogate, for I recognized then that, at least for me, closures could never be casual. During the weeks I share in a client's growth, I usually learn to love her. I truly care what happens to her. I can't turn that love and concern off just because she feels she's able to go on alone.

After I'd concluded the meetings with my very first client, I rather assumed that all of them would be just as wonderful. But I discovered very quickly that each one is different. My second client was from an entirely different mold. Cara and I never felt close. From the start there seemed to be a wall between us. But, even if my relationship with a client isn't good at all, a closure is still necessary. Our last meeting enables us both to rid ourselves of any anger or frustration.

Cara and I had gone through all the prescribed exercises. We had talked—had shared memories and fears. But everything we did seemed mechanical. Nevertheless, we persisted. I was optimistic, and she was convinced that if there was a problem, it was hers and that it would, in time, be solved. After fourteen sessions, we finally faced our difficulty and agreed to discuss it with the therapist. We hadn't made the progress we'd hoped for. By this time, we both recognized that we were beginning to blame each other for the failure.

The therapist passed no judgment. It didn't concern her who might be at fault—or if any fault should even be placed. But her decision was instantaneous. If we still didn't get along, after this length of time, then we should dissolve the relationship. I glanced at Cara. She was as relieved as I. At the therapist's suggestion, we returned to our private room for the closure session.

Now, when neither of us feared it might get in the way of the work at hand, all our animosity came out. Cara spoke first. "You never seemed to be sensitive to my particular needs. I felt as if you were off somewhere else whenever I talked to you."

She picked up steam. "Everything you did was so mechanical. All the exercises were obviously so routine to you." She paused and started again. "But worst of all, you look just like Frank. He was so cruel when we finally broke up. I'll never forget the terrible things he said."

I was ready to respond, but she hurried on. "Most of all, I think, I resented the fact that you had other clients besides me, and you let me know it. I always had the feeling you couldn't wait to leave me and get with someone else."

Now I was sure she was finished. But before I could say a word, she spoke once more. "I guess I resented paying you for doing things that gave you as much if not more pleasure than they gave me. I could see how much you enjoyed giving and getting the sensate-focused body caresses. But while you were getting a kick out of rubbing my body, I barely felt a thing. It just wasn't fair. Besides, if I had a lover, he'd do it for nothing."

I couldn't conceal my own resentment any longer. "If you felt that way, why didn't you go get a man to do the exercises with you? The therapist would have gone along with that."

I didn't wait for an answer. One by one, I answered her accusations and made some of my own. She had been the one who was mechanical when we did the exercises. She was the one who never really listened to my directions and who always did everything wrong. I spoke until I was exhausted, and then she took over. For thirty minutes we talked, criticizing each other without concern for how hurtful we might be, until, finally, all our anger was exhausted. Our eyes met, and we both smiled.

Suddenly, we were laughing openly. "Would you lie down and cuddle for a moment?" I wasn't sure how she'd respond, but I knew I needed to be close before we separated for the last time. Reluctantly, she sat on the bed and then lay down. I lay beside her, one arm under her shoulders, her head resting on my chest. It seemed very natural, even though we were both fully clothed.

"Remember the first time we were nude together?" I smiled as I spoke.

"God, I was so damned mad at you for not having shorts on." Cara was laughing now. "I was sure any man who didn't wear shorts was a sleep-around guy, and I didn't appreciate being assigned to a loose fellow for sex instruction." She chuckled. "I think I was even more mad because it showed you expected we'd be nude and you hadn't felt it necessary to dress completely before coming to me."

"You were embarrassed because it took you so much longer than me to undress. Remember?"

We both laughed again, remembering the awkwardness of that moment.

"Remember when we did the sexological?" Cara turned to face me. "You looked so silly hunting for my uterus. I figured you were supposed to know everything, so I wasn't going to tell you that since I'd had a hysterectomy I didn't have a uterus anymore."

We both laughed at that. And then, for the rest of the next half hour, we talked animatedly, closely, and—surprisingly—lovingly. For the first time since we began working together, I felt that Cara was opening up and letting me get close.

When our time was over, we rose. We'd discussed the bad and the good. We'd dissipated all our unresolved conflicts and had a good laugh in the process. We'd answered all the questions we hadn't even had time to ask before. We did more holding and nurturing in that last session than we had in all the fourteen that had preceded it. Yet we still recognized that we would not be able to work together. Our chemistry, our psyches, and our minds just didn't click.

Cara admitted that if she'd had a man who was willing to do the caressing exercises with her, she wouldn't have come to a surrogate in the first place. She also admitted that she could see how just doing the exercises without the expertise of a surrogate to seek out her problems wouldn't have solved anything.

I finally acknowledged that her attitude had turned me off from the start but that, instead of dealing with it, I had assumed that I'd overcome my reservations as we worked together. And then, after all this, we closed with a wonderful, friendly, if not passionate, hug and kiss. We never saw each other again. But my slate was now clear. I was ready to go on to another client. Because we had taken time for a closure, my memories of her are good and positive.

If I hadn't insisted on this closing session *before* my association with Cara began, I doubt that it would have taken place. When it started, we were too full of animosity. But as it progressed, we mellowed. We realized we would not have to continue to deal with each other. This knowledge allowed us to remain detached even while airing our grievances. Knowing that soon we would no longer intrude on each other's lives, we were able to part as friends.

A closure agreement should always be included in any relationship, especially those that appear more likely, for some reason, to go bad. They are often the ones we back away from and try to pretend never happened. As a surrogate, I've had my share of relationships that didn't quite work out. Surrogates aren't chosen by therapists in the same way one chooses a date. We're picked because the therapist believes we can help the client—and sometimes she's wrong. No one person is going to be a perfect match for everyone else in the world who just happens to be of the opposite sex.

Ginny was another client who didn't work out. I'd been meeting with her for ten sessions when she suddenly informed the therapist that she no longer wanted to work with me. For the three sessions prior to that decision, she'd asked me to observe her with the therapist. I was to remain silent unless spoken to directly and asked to respond. She didn't want me to speak for fear I might influence what she said to the therapist.

On the tenth session she asked me to wait outside for a while. That was when she asked that I be replaced. At the end of that hour, I was called in. Ginny had said she wanted to share her feelings with me. "I never felt we had the kind of rapport we should have had," she began. "Not that I blame you. Sometimes, people just don't hit it off. But I felt we never really got close."

I nodded. I knew she was right there. Our lack of intimacy had bothered me.

"Maybe it was because you're married. I had reservations about that from the start. And then you're a lot older than I am." Again, she was right. I was at least twenty years her senior. Nevertheless, I was convinced that none of these were really the cause of her dismissing me. I had a strong feeling I had been guiding her to where she would have to deal with a lot of problems she feared. Rather than face those very real issues, she chose to back out of surrogate therapy. I was relieved to know that she still intended to continue with her therapist.

When at last my turn came to talk, I admitted that I, too, had felt that we hadn't really hit it off. There'd always been a gap between us which I'd never been able to bridge. I, too, had been uneasy. I felt that she'd never known what it meant to be close. Closeness had always been an important part of my life. When I finished, we both turned to the therapist. I spoke. "May we have a few minutes alone to say good-bye?"

The therapist left us together in the office. We talked for a while, and then something seemed to change in our relationship. When our time was up, we stood and embraced. It was the most emotional, close, touching experience we'd shared in all our time together. Ginny clung to me as she never had before. We both felt ready to cry.

In the short period of closure, we'd become close friends who were saying good-bye forever, not because we *wanted* to, but because we *had* to. Then I left and the therapist returned.

Later, I discussed the closure with the therapist. Both of us were impressed with what had happened. Clearly, the only time this client could establish intimacy with another person was when she was sure that the relationship was at an end. Only then did she feel safe enough to let herself experience emotion. We talked about some of the events in Ginny's life which she had mentioned to me, and they all fit the pattern. She would hold people at arm's length until she felt sure the relationship was at an end. Then she'd feel love and regret at losing a friend. With this information, the therapist was able to go on and, in subsequent weeks, help Ginny to recognize her problem.

Ultimately, Ginny was placed with a younger male surrogate, and then, near the end of her therapy, she consulted an older female surrogate who worked with her in a nonsexual relationship to overcome her negative feelings about her own body. I had no direct part in that treatment, but the therapist and I recognized that if there hadn't been that closure, far more time could have elapsed before she got to the root of Ginny's troubles.

As important as a good closure is when a relationship is *not* ideal, it's even more valuable when two people have been close. In the first chapter, I spoke of how devastating it was for me to lose my first client without having a chance to thank her for all she'd taught me, and to have her express her feelings about the hours we'd spent together. I'd fallen in love with my client, and she with me.

But, sometimes, love isn't as mutual.

I worked for a time with a woman who was in the process of getting a divorce. She and her husband had been through "couple therapy" together, but it hadn't been successful. They did the exercises nicely when they were under the direction of the therapist, but when they got home they fell back into their pattern of arguing and bickering.

The woman, whom I will call Doris, already knew all the exercises, and so we seemed to get along well from the start. What I didn't consider was that, since she and I worked smoothly together and she was in the emotional upheaval of a divorce, she might be more vulnerable than usual. Certainly, I didn't realize that she'd fallen in love with me.

The therapist didn't know, either. Doris had carefully

concealed her emotions and was trying to deal with the problem herself. I was told to focus on her passive attitude and her fear of change. It wasn't that she didn't recognize the necessity of a divorce, but she had never been on her own, never been independent or self-sufficient.

We worked on these areas of her personality. I did a lot of role-playing with her, so she'd be ready to seek employment and not be afraid to go for interviews. I worked on helping her develop her own goals, and to sever her dependency ties with her husband. It was during this period that her feelings toward me came tumbling out.

Fortunately, the therapist caught them in time and was able to deal with them. But they did complicate her therapy. For one thing, Doris insisted that she wanted to continue with me even after her divorce was final, since she'd be alone for the first time and would need support. But the therapist and I both knew that such an arrangement wouldn't be good for her. It would encourage her to transfer her dependency from her ex-husband to me. So it was decided that, since her work with me had actually been completed, we should terminate our relationship.

Doris requested that our closure session be open-ended, so no special time limit would intrude on our farewells. And then we were alone together. That last session was very emotional—and very nonsexual. But it *was* sensuous. Only as we kissed good-bye did I fully realize how much I was going to miss her.

About three weeks later, I received a call from her therapist asking if I'd consent to see Doris one more time in a totally nonsexual setting. She wanted to talk to me once as a friend, with all overtones of teacher/client removed. I agreed.

We spent several hours together in a restaurant. An amazing change had come over her in those few weeks since I had last seen her, and I was delighted. She had found a great new job. She was excited about her future and the adventures that lay ahead. However, at the same time, she admitted to being frightened. Everything was so new to her. But during our closure session she'd recognized how much inner strength she really had. Before that day, she'd been certain she needed me for support. After our closure, she knew that she could take care of herself.

We parted after that dinner and have not seen each other again. But I feel very happy about her. I know she can handle whatever comes along. I remember her as the radiant, happy individual who said good-bye at the restaurant door, and I'm pleased to recall that I contributed to the confidence she now possesses.

All closures can't be as pleasant as that one. And sometimes, in real life, we can't have a closure with a person at all. A spouse dies suddenly, leaving hundreds of words of love unsaid. What can the survivor do, when a closure of the type I've described is impossible?

Psychologists have learned that role-playing can help us fill in those empty places. Just as I devised little games that allowed Doris to practice just how she would act when she applied for a job, a psychologist can work with a client and for a time take on the role of the missing person with whom a closure is needed. It obviously isn't the same as if you could effect the closure with the one you've lost, but you can say what you need to say, and your surrogate can fill in the words you long to hear.

Not all incomplete affairs involve someone who has died. Often, a person's last contact with an ex-lover or ex-spouse is filled with anger and vituperation. In the rush and fury of separation or divorce, no one thinks of the need for properly closing a relationship that had once been loving.

I wonder, sometimes, what would happen if all divorced couples and separated lovers got together one more time, just to close everything off. I suspect that few if any relationships would be reestablished. But what I think *would* happen is that the people who are now encumbered with regrets and angers that have never been voiced would suddenly find themselves free. The past could be put aside at last. Both persons could step out with renewed energy, ready to pick up the pieces of life that had been kept in disarray just because some previous relationship had not been properly concluded.

12

OPENING THE DOOR
TO THE FUTURE
Raising Emotionally Healthy Children

Y ears ago, when I was taking a graduate
course in child psychology, a few other class
members and I were given an interesting assignment—to
observe several teachers working with autistic children.
Youngsters with this affliction seem unaware of the world
around them—neither seeing nor hearing what takes
place in their presence. Some never recognize their sur-
roundings or the people with whom they deal every day.
Their entire attention seems to be focused on something
inside themselves.

One pretty little girl spent most of her time with an
imaginary pitcher in her hand, holding it under an imaginary water faucet and then filling an imaginary cup. She
was oblivious to everyone and everything around her. I
felt sad watching her go through this daily ritual while
the teachers attempted to help her. It appeared to me
that they were totally ineffective in dealing with her problem.

Then, one day, one of the teachers settled down beside
the child and took her in her arms. From that time on, at
every opportunity, she stroked the child's head, ca-

176

ressed her face, or touched her in some way. Often, she just held her. Unfortunately, there seemed to be no reaction to this new form of contact. While she was being held, the child remained absolutely quiet. But as soon as she was released, she returned to her water game as if nothing had happened.

Some days later, while the teacher was working with another child, the pretty girl wandered over toward her. Even though it seemed highly unlikely, she appeared to be waiting in line for attention.

The next day, the same thing happened. Now, I sensed, a pattern was developing. Was it really possible that this child who never noticed anything was actively seeking love?

On our last day as observers, the child walked up to the teacher and stood beside her. The teacher faced the child, knelt down, and turned on the imaginary faucet for her. The little girl looked into the woman's eyes for a moment or two and then put her imaginary pitcher under that nonexistent faucet until it was full. Suddenly, the pitcher was forgotten. The girl wrapped her arms around the teacher's neck and began to weep. For the first time in her six years of life, she had recognized and communicated with another human being.

It was then that I first fully understood the tremendous power of touch.

I was reminded of that experience years later when I was teaching at the Center. A psychotherapist approached me with a request. She had been working with a sex offender who had been given a choice by the court. Either he go into therapy or return to jail. Naturally, he had chosen the former. Now his therapist wanted to know how I felt about including him in my class.

"He isn't a violent man," she assured me. "Luke's offense is exhibitionism and voyeurism. I think if he could interact with normal people in a structured environment including nudity, intimacy, and caring, he might find something he needs."

After discussing the question with my co-leader, I agreed to let Luke join the group. We decided not to tell the other members about his particular problem. In itself, that isn't unusual. Many class members prefer not to share much about themselves at the beginning of the classes. Only after they learn to be intimate do they reveal their reasons for coming to the Center at all.

In these enrichment classes, we undertake many of the same exercises I do with my clients, and so, sooner or later, we find it necessary to be nude together. Before that session, we talk about how, in our society, we usually equate being nude and touching with sex. We discuss the problems that many people have when they try to separate the two ideas, and how often we reject all touch because we fear it *has* to lead to sex. We point out that each one of us has a personal "touching limit" which we consider acceptable.

This having been said, we encourage the students to expand their own limits and options. For example, one woman was comfortable when her hands were caressed but upset when anyone touched her face. We worked with her until she could accept both face touching and embracing without fearing that anything more would happen.

As we begin the session requiring nudity, we ask each class member how he or she feels about disrobing. This time, as usual, some of our members were uneasy while others were comfortable. Luke, however, was beside himself with glee. When we had all undressed and formed a standing circle, Luke was the only man who had an immediate, full erection.

In all the years I've been associated with group and social nudity, I've rarely seen a man with an erection. Most men are too embarrassed or apprehensive the first time, and after that they realize there's nothing inherently sexual about being naked.

There are, of course, some exceptions. Young men and teenagers who might not be in control of their reactions may respond to public nudity at a nudist camp by having erections. Men whose visions of nudity always include sex fantasies may also have problems. And men who suffer deep psychological problems may certainly find social nudity difficult to manage.

I don't mean to imply that a man is psychologically defective because he gets an occasional erection in a nude group. But I do wish to make the point that it's a rare occurrence. Even if a man wakes at a nudist camp and has his usual morning erection, he finds that it subsides quickly because of the number of people around him who are involved in nonsexual activities.

Of course, Luke's erection was obvious to us all. A few class members seemed intrigued, and some may even have shared his arousal, but most of the others were uncomfortable. Luke, however, seemed not the least embarrassed. He appeared to be enjoying his difference and his awareness of the response he was getting from the women in the group.

This is typical of exhibitionists. They get sexual satisfaction from the response of their "victims." Shock, surprise, and even disgust shown by the observer gives them pleasure. I've since spoken to a few such men, and they tell me they secretly fantasize that the sight of their erection will elicit an invitation to sex from a viewer. However, they acknowledge that were a woman to offer herself to them, they'd probably lose the erection before any intimate contact could occur. Most prefer to masturbate while recalling the expression of horror that their exposure elicited.

I made no immediate reference to Luke, nor did my fellow instructor. Instead, I began my customary speech. "We all have tacit permission to look at any part of the others in the room, and to be looked at in turn. We'll start by studying each other's eyes and faces." Each time we moved our focus down, I discussed the differences between individuals and between males and females.

When we got to our groins, I continued, "We men have penises that are different sizes. Mine is thinner than Jack's. Roger's is longer, even when it's flaccid. Luke is the only one who has an erection."

As soon as he realized that the men as well as the women were looking at him, Luke lost his erection. With no further comment, I continued with the exercise.

Luke continued to have erections in subsequent classes. During the first touching exercise, he once more became aroused. Mostly for his benefit, but also for general information, I remarked that many of us were taught from childhood to believe that if we touched another naked body, we would automatically be aroused. "It's okay if that happens to you. But under no circumstances are you to do anything about it. Just enjoy the feeling in your own body, but don't inflict your reactions on your partner and don't do anything sexual."

When Luke found that he was being treated like all the others in the class, he gradually lost his tendency to get an erection as soon as he was nude. He realized that he was recognized as an equal member of the group whether he was aroused or not. The state of his penis didn't affect how others reacted to him. I learned later that this was the first time Luke had ever been accepted by others so openly. It had been part of his problem that he felt rejected by everyone he met.

During the rest of the sessions I noticed more about him. He was more reluctant to touch someone than any of the other men. If a woman approached him for an embrace, he accepted it. But he never approached anyone himself. Also, once his erections stopped, he began to walk around with a towel covering his genitals. He seemed to be embarrassed, and he was very careful to avoid any close contact with other men.

At our last session, as we were saying our good-byes, Luke came to me and asked if he could have a hug. Other class members soon gathered around us, and his final act as a member of the group was to hug and be hugged by everyone, men and women alike.

I never saw Luke again, but the therapist who worked with him told me that he is still out of jail. I'm not implying that twelve weeks of a class on self-acceptance and sensual expression solved all his problems, but I do feel that the touching, a natural part of the class work, gave him something important in his life that he had been missing.

This set me to remembering the little girl I'd watched at the class for autistic children. It had been painful for me to see her and her classmates so unresponsive to human contact. Was there so great a difference between them and Luke? They ignored the world full of people outside themselves. He pictured others in a way that was totally unrealistic. Both the children and Luke were substituting inner visions of the world for its reality.

Like many people who work in health and paramedical fields, I treasure the goal of reaching a level in societal development where people are open and honest with one another. In such a society, most present-day social services would not be needed. As a natural adjunct to that dream, I find myself wondering why, when we all start out with the fresh, open minds of infants, we develop into such unhappy, isolated people.

While I've had limited contact with children (I work exclusively with adults), my experience with my own children and with clients who are parents has given me some insight into what we do to become what we are. One mistake we make is to isolate sexual expression and not talk about it to our children. Nearly every client I've had who's been the parent of a daughter has expressed regret that she wasn't more open about sex to her child. It is, certainly, the subject most carefully avoided by many parents. Often, they simply feel they don't know enough about it to teach their children. They ignore the issue entirely, and in so doing they convince their children that it's probably the most important thing in their lives.

In my family, we discussed sex openly with our children, but we gave it no more and no less attention than we gave to any other subject. Because we never treated our discussions about sex as if they were any different from our talks about school, grades, proper eating habits, and many other important areas of our children's lives, they never developed a fixation on sex as something very different or unusual.

Schools today have sex-education classes. However, they deal only with the nuts and bolts of the subject, not with the emotions involved in this important aspect of our lives. Educators evidently feel that it's the parents' responsibility to teach such intimate aspects of sex. But most parents, afraid of making a mistake or just afraid of the subject in general, say nothing at all to their children. Many parents assume that schools are handling the entire subject.

My belief is that it isn't so much *who* teaches or *what* is taught, but rather *how* it is handled. What happens now is a travesty. In many elementary schools, girls are herded into the auditorium and shown a bad film accompanied by a poor lecture on menstruation. Boys are excluded. This very decision to keep boys from knowing what is happening to their female classmates isolates them from female sexuality. Boys, too, are given classes on sex, with an emphasis on how males develop. Each sex learns something about the other, but they're always taught separately, as if what one sex knows is not fit for the other's ears.

Parents are often embarrassed and hesitant when they give their children sex instruction. Much of the time, when a father is ready to talk about sex to his son, the child has already picked up the rudiments on the street. And, because of the school classes, most children today know far more about the mechanics of reproduction than their parents ever did at a similar age. But they know little or nothing about the humanity of it—about the emotions surrounding the sex act. They aren't acquainted with closeness or loving or caring or responsibility.

When I asked a group of teenagers if they'd like to have a class on sexuality taught in school, the results were mixed. Several thought it would take too much time. Many felt it would be too embarrassing if boys and girls were taught together, as I suggested. A few liked the idea. But the most unnerving response came from a charming sixteen-year-old girl. "Oh, we already know all about sex," she announced. "We saw a film on menstruation, and we learned all about where babies come from in our health class."

To say that her words frightened me is an understatement. She thought she knew it all. But she and her fellows know only the most basic facts. They know what is needed to procreate, but they know nothing about sharing affection or giving pleasure. They're ignorant of the ramifications of human sexual interaction.

A young woman psychologist summed up her feelings in my presence, and I found myself agreeing heartily with her. "When kids are growing up, they sense and accept the feelings and attitudes their parents have toward life far more than they accept the words they hear. When we talk about integrity, honor, love, and respect, we're talking about vague concepts. But if parents are true role models, and if their behavior conforms to their attitudes, the kids learn more than they ever could from all the lectures in the world."

Children today are scared. They know where babies come from and how they're made, but many of them are still afraid that masturbation will make hair grow on the palms of their hands. Most girls know about herpes and the danger of becoming pregnant, but they don't understand their body's reaction when a boy they like is nearby. Far too many parents and sex educators are afraid that if they give children too much knowledge *about* sex, they're also giving them tacit permission to *have* sex. They believe that if they explain birth control to a teen or preteen girl, she may assume they're suggesting she immediately take proper precautions and, if she does, they'll then approve of her having intercourse.

What children should learn about sex are those things immediately affecting them. They need to understand how each individual develops at a different pace. One girl may mature at eleven, another not until she's seventeen. Yet both are normal. They need to be taught understanding of these differences. The early developer shouldn't be mocked and teased because of her breasts or made to feel odd because she's menstruating. Neither should the late developer be made to feel that she's backward or slow. They both need to be helped to accept each other and to appreciate the little tomboy who, thirteen and menstruating, is still happier playing baseball than joining with her peers in pursuits generally classified as feminine. And all girls need to learn enough about male development so they're prepared to cope with the behavior of boys who are reaching puberty.

Boys, too, need to recognize that they're not all the same and to understand that different behavior doesn't make one boy less masculine than another. A young lad may hear his peers talking about "beating your meat" and wonder, as I did, what pleasure there could be in hitting one's penis with a fist. Boys who are slow in reaching puberty may find all discussion of sex confusing. Because someone else may already be experienced in masturbation techniques, a slow developer is apt to feel less worthy. So boys, like girls, need to be helped to understand the variable rate at which different people develop.

Because I was a boy myself, I am aware of how cruel boys can be when they meet a child who is small or different. I remember how, when I was at this stage, all the boys I knew worried about their penis size. But since we had no real basis for comparison, we usually kept our worries to ourselves.

When he was very young, my son came home in tears one day because some older boys had taunted him. He was so skinny. How could he ever be a man with such small muscles? I felt fortunate that he came to me, for I was able to show him a photograpah of myself at his age, and I was even smaller than he was. Reassured, he returned to his play.

Not only should children be prepared for the unintentional cruelty of their playmates, they also need to understand the effect that their physical development may have on others. Girls, for example, seem, by nature, to be lovable, sweet, caressable little children. As they grow up, they're hugged by both parents. Their fathers, who tend to be more physical, may possibly indulge in a bit of roughhousing with them, much the same as is done with young boys.

Then the girl begins to develop breasts. Suddenly, the father seems to have a change of attitude. He no longer roughhouses with his daughter. He treats her with a kind of diffidence that confuses her. What's happened? Is she less worthy of her father's love because she now looks like a woman? Are women somehow not as desirable as girls and boys? She wonders why she couldn't just remain a little girl and still be happy and loved.

Mothers now take over in teaching their daughters what they will need to know about life, but far too frequently they, themselves, are very badly informed. By this time the girl may have received the sex education provided by the schools. She knows the mechanics of sex, but she gets her attitudes toward herself and her relationships with men from her mother, who got *her* information from *her* mother—on back into the distant past.

Despite the many books written about the sharing of pleasure in sex and the many advances that have been made by women's rights groups, many mothers today are still teaching their daughters attitudes toward life that were popular at the turn of the century—that, for example, sex is something men need and women put up with. As a result, far too many of today's women still approach life with attitudes straight from 1905—or earlier.

Lest we assume the boys are faring better, we need to consider what happens as a boy matures. Back in the early part of the century, it was common for fathers to take their maturing sons to a brothel, where an understanding woman would teach them the rudiments of sex. Much of the time, they learned only the procedure for insertion and orgasm—*their* orgasm.

Today, boys may be even worse off. They're expected to get their knowledge from books. Often, they learn to think of sex as simply mechanical. Certain acts are performed, like hugging and stroking, then the penis goes into the vagina and the man begins to pump. No one teaches boys to consider the emotional aspects of intimate relationships.

The result of poor instruction and these antiquated attitudes is that girls often grow up frightened of sex and boys grow up thinking that sex is something they must have at any cost. Unfortunately, that cost is often the emotional welfare of the women they encounter.

The present-day media blitz dealing with sex might be assumed to have eliminated all the problems we've inherited from the past. But consider what most films dealing with sex have to say. Almost all the more acceptable films (not X-rated) are concerned with titillation, hidden thrills, and secret acts. And bodies. They're filled with disguised hints about the thrills that are available with the opposite sex. They emphasize the importance of certain physical attributes, like beauty (which is very stereotyped) and being attractive to others.

I'll bet I could count on the fingers of one hand the number of times I've seen a sex-instruction film that dealt with real caring and the sharing of emotions. I know I've seen even fewer that illustrate the value of vulnerability and sensitivity in personal relationships. We see toothy smiles and oiled bodies that dash about in tiny strips of cloth, which we are subliminally informed are the epitome of sexiness. Then our children turn and look at the people around them and become convinced that they must not be like their parents if they ever want to be sexy and desirable.

For us adults, this dichotomy creates enough problems. We dream of how wonderful life would be if only our partner looked like Farrah or Loni—or Robert or Tom. It's no wonder that many of us can't communicate. In our fantasies, we're talking to Tom or Farrah, but we're being heard by far more ordinary people. We may even believe, since we too are ordinary, that we're valueless. It's clear that we don't fit the picture of real sexiness portrayed in the media.

But if we adults have problems, consider what these messages tell our children. They strive with all their young energy to become carbon copies of the latest rock stars, and when they fail, or when their parents protest at their bizarre clothing and odd hairstyles and force them to conform to less modern patterns, they feel devalued. They're convinced that they can never achieve the degree of sexiness needed to make them feel worthwhile.

What can we do to help our children? Obviously, I recognize that the concept of a *Sexual* Enrichment Experience for teenagers is much too shocking for most of our society to accept. But how about a *Human* Enrichment Experience to supplement public school sex education? The word *sex* doesn't even have to be mentioned. In this Human Enrichment Experience, boys and girls would be helped to talk about how they feel. Guided by experienced, understanding adults, the girls in one room and the boys in another would first discuss things they might consider too private to talk about in mixed company.

The girls could talk about how it feels to have breasts when most other girls don't yet have them—or how it feels to be flat-chested when your friends are all budding out. They could talk openly about how they react when a boy touches them. What urges are stirred up when they fantasize? What can they do if a boy tries to rush them into having sex? How can they say no and still keep his friendship? What are boys really saying when they act extra macho? Who are boys trying to impress when they claim they've "made it" with a girl and they actually haven't?

Boys could discuss penis size and what it feels like to be aroused. They could face and settle forever the old fable that if a man gets an erection and doesn't immediately have an orgasm, he'll have "blue balls." What happens when girls menstruate? How do girls react when they're mauled, or when boys grab at them? Why are girls so confusing? Why do girls dress so revealingly? Why do some girls tease boys and get them all excited and then back off?

Then, one more meeting could be held with boys and girls together. Now, guided by their two caring, knowledgeable instructors, they could discuss feelings. What do parents really want from their kids? What do teachers think about them? How can they get along better with their peers?

In this large mixed gathering, there wouldn't have to be any touching. But they could *talk* about touching, as well as other subjects. Why do we react as we do when our bodies touch? What does it feel like to kiss? What is normal in body size and shape, and what would be a normal psychological attitude toward sex and sexuality? What's the difference between sexuality and sensuality? What do we mean when we talk of caring and sharing? What is intimacy? Why is it important to respect other people's bodies and accept the fact that we all mature at different rates? Why, since intercourse is not only a natural act but fun as well, are teenagers advised not to do it? What are the responsibilities that accompany sex? If the possibility of pregnancy is taken care of through contraceptives, isn't it okay then? Why not?

Ideally, I would prefer that there be an opportunity for *some* touching—done with guidance—so the boys and girls could learn to distinguish between various kinds of physical contact. What, for example, is the difference between "copping a feel" and affectionate caressing? When sexual urges are strong, as they are in teenage boys, they often grab what they want. Yet this is the proper time to show them the value of caring, nurturing, and loving.

I'm not suggesting that these classes be compulsory. Like the classes in the mechanics of sex, they can be voluntary. But they should be scheduled on a regular basis, just like any other elective. There shouldn't be special attention given to them. For that matter, I think the fuss made over the *present* sex-education classes only puts abnormal emphasis on them.

One of the main goals of these Human Enrichment classes should be to help children recognize that there's nothing intrinsically wrong with intercourse. Every parent in the world has indulged in it. But we want our children to know there's a right *time* and a right *place* for sex, and a right *person* as well. Sexuality, like integrity and honesty, requires a great deal of personal responsibility.

I know a woman who never denied her children when they asked for a taste of alcohol, because she didn't want them to feel it was important enough to develop a craving for it. In her case, at least, she achieved her goal. Her sons, adults now, accept some alcohol with meals, but they aren't addicted to it. They don't think it's special.

I wish we dared follow such a concept when we teach our children about sex. For the foreseeable future, that would be impossible. But I'd like to see one addition to the Human Enrichment Experience I've already described. I would like to add a special day when, under careful adult supervision, the teenagers had an opportunity to observe and touch one another's nude bodies so they could learn not only how to pleasure *themselves*, but also how touching affects another person.

I'm not sure that a girl can comprehend the sheer lust felt by a teenage boy with an erection. And I doubt any boy understands how a girl feels when her menstrual period begins. But I do know both could develop compassion for the other. I know the boy needs to learn to contain his urge. I know the girl and the boy could both gain from such intimate sharing as might take place in this kind of group. Perhaps, as in the adult Sexual Enrichment Experience, touch could be divorced from sex, so the teenagers could recognize the effect of shared touching and thereby develop the mutual understanding that is far too often lacking in adult sexual acts. Maybe then, today's teenagers could grow up to be far better adjusted and far happier than their predecessors.

Were this to happen, there would probably be little need for sex therapists or surrogates. But I wouldn't regret the loss of my profession. I'd rejoice, knowing that the misunderstanding and misinformation which, in the past, had produced isolated, uneasy people who didn't dare reach out to others, had finally been put behind us. And I'd look forward to a new, peaceful future. Wouldn't it be wonderful to see how this new ability on the part of each individual to relate to others might affect the affairs of the world?

13

YOU CAN DO IT
Dare to Be Intimate

There are as many kinds of sexual problems as there are people. Some are easily overcome once the two partners begin to communicate. Others aren't solved so quickly. If you and your chosen partner are having sexual difficulties that involve impotence or frigidity, premature ejaculation or the inability to reach orgasm, I strongly advise you to seek professional help. There are qualified sex therapists throughout the world who are capable of helping you deal with such conditions. If you need to work with a surrogate, you can find one of them, too.

But, you may say, what precisely is it a surrogate does that you can't do for yourself? Why should you hire a surrogate when you have a lover or a spouse to work with you?

These are certainly legitimate questions. We would generally agree that couples should work together. Therapists prefer this arrangement. After all, problems are seldom one-sided. You both share the responsibility if you're not communicating. But, occasionally, something affects us as we grow up—something that makes us incapable of accepting intimacy. Then, in spite of our love for our partners, we build roadblocks that keep us apart.

Homer and Lila provide an excellent example of this kind of interference with good communication. They also illustrate the value of professional help, for without the assistance of a good sex therapist, their marriage most probably would have ended in divorce.

These two people had been married for thirty years. They had much in common, including children who had grown up and formed families of their own. Now they were alone, and they decided to do something about their constant bickering, which had been bad for years and seemed to grow worse each day. Each complained about the other's touch and amorous approach, and so they very seldom had sex, even though they both felt strong urges. They'd been through therapy of all kinds but had never experienced more than temporary improvement. Despite everything, they continued to argue and fight. So they enlisted the aid of a sex therapist.

When the therapist sent them off to a separate room to try an exercise in sensate focus, they were delighted. But after a few minutes of silence, their voices could be heard through the closed door. "No, you have it all wrong," Lila shouted. "That's not how you're supposed to do it." The door swung open and she stormed out. "Why can't you do anything right, Homer? You just don't know how to touch me."

Eventually, because Homer didn't seem to be getting the idea, they both agreed that he should work with a surrogate. After he'd had five or six sessions with his new partner, it was Lila who didn't seem to know what she was doing. Homer insisted that everything was fine as long as he was with his substitute companion.

In self-defense, Lila decided she needed a surrogate, too. It was then I was called in. Since she'd already gone through all the sensate exercises, we got right down to the nitty-gritty, and, to my surprise, I found her to be a warm, loving, caring, orgasmic woman.

I spoke to the surrogate who was working with Homer. She insisted that he was a fine, lovable, caring, warm, potent, and orgasmic man. We were confused. If that was true, what was the problem? We decided to try them together once more.

The bickering began even before they were alone. The therapist, the other surrogate, and I could, at last, see the problem. They both knew what they were *supposed* to do and how they were *supposed* to feel, but every time they got near each other they were so preoccupied with all the garbage from their past that they couldn't reach an understanding.

Finally, in desperation, the therapist came up with a new approach. She contacted several other therapists, two surrogates, and one of Homer and Lila's friends. We all got together in a large room, undressed, and spread a towel on the floor. Lila was told to lie down on her stomach, close her eyes, and just enjoy. Then we all knelt around her, poured oil on our hands, and, with Homer, began to give her a tender, loving, sensate-focused back caress.

Every so often, one of us would ask Lila how her back felt, what she wanted us to do, and where the touching seemed best. She would answer, "Oh, that hand on the back of my neck feels real warm and loving," or "That hand on the small of my back feels great," or "That person who's touching my legs really knows how to make me feel good." And when she answered, we would look at the person who was touching that spot. Invariably, it was Homer.

This was decidedly unusual. After about ten or twelve minutes of such group back caressing, most people can't tell the difference between the many fingers and hands that participate. They can't even tell whether a man or a woman is touching any particular spot. But every time Lila spoke of hands that felt especially good, she referred to the place where Homer was touching her. *Every time.* It was always Homer's hands that felt best, Homer's touch that brought about the most pleasant response.

Finally, most of us stopped, leaving only the hands she had informed us felt best. Then we told her to open her eyes and look around to see whose hands they were. The expression on her face brought tears to our eyes. After a brief pause, the therapist spoke. "Forget the past. You can see it makes no difference to your bodies that you've had misunderstandings. Stay in the present and consider what has just occurred. Homer knows how to touch you, Lila. Your body recognizes that. It's your mind that needed to be convinced." Then we all rose and left them alone.

When they emerged from the privacy of their room some sixty minutes later, they were smiling. Lila was at last able to see that, for her, Homer was the greatest lover in the world. They were both very grateful, for they realized that they could not have reached this new understanding without help. The therapist and the surrogates and their friend had all played a part in their lesson.

I don't mean to say that closeness and intimacy can only be achieved with a surrogate. If you have a basically good relationship that seems only to be fading in interest, and if you are looking for something that will serve to bring back your past feelings of fun and excitement at being together, there are things you can do, new ways of communicating that you can explore. If you long for the touching and closeness that was important when you first came together, some of the exercises we surrogates do with our clients may help you renew your feeling of intimacy.

Let's begin with a typical situation in a couple's life. You've both had a hard day at work. After dinner, your partner seems exhausted, but you've been dreaming all day about making love. You want action, and you want it now.

You certainly have the right to ask for anything you want. But your partner also has the right to refuse. Yet, if you ask and are summarily rejected, nothing has been done to increase your feelings of closeness. On the contrary, with just a short question and answer you've built a chasm which neither one of you can cross.

However, there is a way to avoid that kind of abrupt end to hopes for intimacy. The way in which a question—and its reply—are phrased can sometimes make all the difference. Then, even if your goals are far apart, you can negotiate. You haven't closed the door in your partner's face.

Suppose you're the husband and you want to make love. If your wife rejects your overtures and states, "Not tonight, Henry, I have a headache," she's brought the matter to a crashing halt. You feel rejected, and a battle may begin. But if she's aware of and concerned with your feelings, she can respond a bit differently.

Instead of the blunt refusal, she might say, "Gee, darling, I know how you feel, and I wish I felt the same way, but I just don't think I'm up to making love tonight. I have a splitting headache. What I really want is to be held and cuddled. Maybe, if you rubbed my shoulders and back, I'd feel better and we might be able to satisfy both of our needs."

This is an example of negotiating that could work just as well in the opposite direction. Suppose you flop on the sofa and lie there, watching your favorite sport on TV.

Your wife sits down beside you, ruffles your hair, and strokes your shoulder. You could push her hand aside and growl, "Stop that! Can't you see I'm watching the game?" But if you do, she's bound to be hurt. Maybe next time you feel amorous, she'll get even.

There's a better way for you to enjoy the program and still not reject your wife. You can kiss her lightly and put your arms around her. "Honey, this is really an exciting game. I'd love to cuddle with you, but do you mind if I watch it for a while first?" By holding her in your arms, you show that you want her near. And your explanation lets her know you'd appreciate having her sit beside you. What could have been total rejection and the basis for later arguments has turned into communication and negotiation.

Not only is it valuable for you to be considerate when you say no to your partner, it's also important to recognize that communication about your sex preferences can sometimes lead to a new and wonderful understanding.

I know a woman who had always resented the rush with which most of her partners hurried to orgasm. For years she'd put up with it, assuming all men were like that. Finally, she mustered her courage and decided that she'd at least tell her next partner what she really wanted, even if speaking out only served to chase him away. But the next man she became involved with was having sexual problems of his own. He had trouble getting an erection. He needed far more time for full arousal than most women permitted him.

These two seemed made for each other. He liked the kissing, touching, and closeness as much as he liked his final orgasm. With my friend, he was able to allow himself to take pleasure in the process of arousal. Because she had dared to speak out, their problems revealed themselves to be blessings in disguise.

What they accomplished was more than a sexual adjustment. They achieved real trust. They became truly intimate because they'd been honest enough to admit their problems. But if she had not dared to speak her mind, and if they had been unwilling to talk about their handicaps, they would never have reached the understanding that added so much to both their lives.

Usually, by the time people admit a sex problem exists, they've been living with it for some time. It's permeated their lives, affecting everything they do and see and think. It's become a focal point of their existence. Everything seems to revolve around it.

For example, if a man has trouble with impotence, it can have a devastating effect on his behavior and self-image. He may not dare to approach a woman. He may consider himself worthless and ineffective in all his activities. Similarly, a woman who's afraid to come near a man sexually because she believes he'll hurt her may gradually find herself avoiding all physical contact. Her isolation and loneliness will be of her own making. Both these people will suffer greatly restricted lives because they're afraid to expose their frailties.

I remarked at the start of this book that to be open to intimacy, one must learn to accept one's own vulnerability. I noted that, for many surrogates, this is achieved during classes in sexual enrichment. But can this vulnerability be developed without attending special classes? I'm not sure, but I think it can.

Most of us have built up a facade that we believe is acceptable to others, a facade behind which we hide our inner thoughts, fears, and desires. We feel safe and comfortable only when we're protected by this wall. Therefore, if we decide to change and become more open, we shouldn't expect miracles. A lifetime habit can't be broken in one day, or one week, or even in one year. It takes time. But each step we take in the direction of being more open with others makes the following steps easier. We were all vulnerable and open when we began life. We should therefore be able to get back at least some of the attitudes that make children so delightful.

When I start working with a client, I ask only that she be willing to hug me and let me touch her hands. I even put a pillow on her lap so I won't accidentally come in contact with her legs. We don't progress to the next step until she's ready. Even though she wants to break through her wall of isolation, I know she must do it gradually.

If you recognize a need in yourself for more contact with others, and with your own feelings, begin slowly. Don't assume that just your decision to change is enough. You need to retrain your mind and your body. You need to regain the openness all babies have at birth. You need to recapture some of your wonder at life, your awareness of your five senses, and your appreciation of all they tell you about the world.

Begin with your sense of touch. Whatever you encounter, take time to become fully aware of how it feels. This is an exercise we did early in my surrogate training, but it doesn't have to be done with an instructor. Feel your clothing. Each garment has a different texture. Experience the smoothness of the paint surface on your car, the roughness of the leather around the steering wheel. Let your toes wiggle in the sand underfoot when you walk on the beach. Note the crispness of some leaves and the softness of others. Make a tactile collection of the textures you gather. At the end of the day, try to recall as many new feelings as you can.

Years ago, I had a little poodle named Bijou who used to get her greatest pleasure from chasing after stones. Most of the time she seemed to find and bring back the exact stone I tossed, even if it landed on a pile of rocks. But never, in the first ten years of her life, had I bothered to notice why she brought back some and not others.

The week after I was introduced to the value of feeling, I was sitting on the lawn under a tree, running my fingers through the grass. I was acutely aware of the tree bark against my back. My bare feet touched a patch of dirt, and I sensed the difference between that contact and the crispness of my trousers against my legs. Looking around to make sure no one else was watching, I picked up a stone and began to fondle it. It was rough, with sharp points and delicate ridges. Bijou sniffed at me and I tossed it for her to fetch.

She chased it, sniffed it, picked it up, then put it down again without bringing it back to me. I picked up another stone and tossed it. This one she returned promptly.

Intrigued, I began to pay more attention to the feel of the stones I threw. Bijou carried back to me only the stones that were smooth, well-rounded, and contoured to fit her mouth. It was her sense of feel that caused her to return certain stones and leave others where they fell.

Animals live daily with a vital sense of touch. We humans, on the other hand, have generally come to rely more on our vision and have somewhat ignored our tactile abilities. But by depressing this important sense, we've become less responsive to all sensations.

As I began to appreciate the feel of everything from a doorknob to a piece of sandpaper, I realized how long I'd neglected that ability. I expanded my awareness to include people. When I shook hands with a woman, I touched her elbow or her wrist as well. That extra contact increased my feeling of sensuousness—and her response.

Finally, I dared to use the same approach when I greeted men. Sometimes they were more friendly, even though they didn't realize what I was doing. But the extra contact meant a lot to me. I seemed to get a clearer picture of the kind of person I was greeting than I did when I limited my touch to a mere handshake.

Now I began to hug women when I greeted them. Not bear hugs, just gentle embraces. One woman remarked that it felt good, but others drew back, almost visibly recoiling, at my approach. As I came to know these women better, I recognized their loneliness and isolation. They didn't dare communicate intimately with anyone. I could sense their unhappiness.

I tried talking more with them, exposing my vulnerability so they would dare to open up to me in turn. With some, I had limited success. Others needed more than I could offer in the casual give-and-take of friendship. Yet, in some cases, they have become more aware of their needs because of my attempts to get close.

If your goal is to increase your own sensitivity, gradually expand the awareness that has started with touching so as to include the other senses. Pay attention to the smells of the city, the fragrance of salt water, and the perfume of flowers. Really see the colors of a sunrise or sunset. Listen for the cricket's chirrup in your backyard. Take time to enjoy the variety of tastes available on your table.

When you're comfortable with this enriched view of the world, expand your awareness of the here and now to include honest responses to questions. If someone asks how you feel, don't give a flip answer. That doesn't mean you should be long-winded or complaining. But if you're worried about something, be willing to talk about it to someone you love. You may have to start with little things. It's a heady experience to give your trust to another human being. You may not be ready to do that for some time. But you have to start somewhere. Cultivate a friend or two with whom you feel safe and slowly begin to open up.

You'll discover something very interesting. Many times, when you and your friend begin to talk about the same event, you'll find you've seen it quite differently. The view we have of reality is rooted in our own personal traditions. A woman whose mother considered sex dirty, something a wife does only to please her husband, will have different feelings about intimacy than a woman whose mother was open in her expressions of love, both to her children and to her husband.

I'm reminded of a hostess who served ham at a gathering I attended. Someone noticed a large chunk had been cut from the ham before it was baked. "Why do you do that?" she asked.

Our hostess shrugged. "That's the way to bake hams. I do it the way my mother showed me."

Fortunately, her mother was present. "That's the way I *always* did it," she remarked. She turned to face *her* mother, who, now close to ninety, was still a spry, active participant in these family gatherings. "You taught me, remember?"

Grandmother smiled. "I never realized you didn't understand. When I was young and you were watching me cook, we only had a small pot for baking. I had to cut up the ham to get it in." She was laughing by the time she finished, and so were we.

But, in a way, her story wasn't funny. It illustrates how we far too often handle our lives. We accept without question attitudes that were valid two generations ago. If you want to improve, you need to find out why you do what you do. Sometimes, just recognizing that you're following an outdated tradition is all that's necessary to bring about change.

I believe that if each of us practiced increasing our

awareness of the world around us through touching, hearing, tasting, smelling, and seeing, we'd not only get in touch with ourselves but with others, too. We'd begin to understand the fears and worries that blight the lives of our loved ones. We'd seek greater closeness and, in that closeness, we'd find solace and healing.

Far too few couples allow themselves this kind of pleasure. They seldom touch unless they decide to have sex, and from that moment on they're in a race to the finish. Everything they do is geared toward the big O. What happens on the way is barely noticed. They even refuse to give names to their actions or to the parts of the body they're touching.

One exercise we sometimes do in classes and with clients is to present a list of words, all medically proper, that denote various parts of the body or the various kinds of sex acts. We ask for as many synonyms as possible for each word. Many people react with horror when first confronted with this exercise. Sometimes, even the medical terminology is too strong for them. But, after we've gone through the list and discussed the many synonyms, their sensitivity seems to vanish. The most disgusting terms lose their shock value when they're dealt with openly and matter-of-factly. And clients' lives seem to open up when they let go of inhibitions that have caused them to reject even the *words* that deal with sex.

Jane, an English teacher, had consistently refused to instruct teenagers. Among other things, she just couldn't stand their vulgarity. But after therapy, she specifically sought out these kids to teach. As she delved, with her students, into the meanings of words and how they originated, she recognized that by denying the existence of all sexual words, she'd actually been denying her own sexuality. She didn't suddenly begin to use four-letter words in everyday speech. Not at all. But she was aware of their impact on her sex life, and she no longer tried to deny their existence.

I'm not advocating the use of "dirty" words. But as Jane said, after she began using earthy terms during intercourse, "I was thinking them, so why not say them? If it wasn't shocking to have sex, why should it be shocking to give a name to what we did?" Sexy words in the proper setting can be as arousing as touch or smell or sight.

Why worry about four-letter words at all? Because as important as it is for us to renew our sensitivity to touch, smell, taste, hearing, and sight, it's equally important that we *desensitize* ourselves to things sexual so we no longer deal with sex as if it were removed from our other life experiences, as if sexual touch differed intrinsically from regular touching.

As I start the sensate-focused body caress exercise with a client, I sometimes find she's very tense and afraid. She lies rigidly with her arms at her sides, fists clenched. I ignore her anxiety and begin by massaging her forehead. As I move down her body, caressing her face, her neck and shoulders, her breasts and ribs, her stomach and genitals, her legs and feet, I take pleasure for myself. I can feel her relax as I move along. And though she might tense up again as I approach her breasts or genitals, when I give them no more attention than any other part of her body, she becomes totally at ease. By the time I finish, any fears or apprehensions she might have had at the start are gone. Because I am enjoying what I do, she can relax and take pleasure in my caressing.

When she takes the active role, she's already learned from me to do what gives her pleasure. She's learned to respect the process and use it herself. She's learned that taking pleasure to give it helps her to accept her own feelings and emotions. Many months later, she will recognize how her ability to take pleasure in touching has released her sexual energy. Sex for her will have ceased to be exclusively a genital activity. It will have become an expression of her entire body, her complete self.

Couples who have sex problems can be embroiled in a contest each time they get together. He may start with, "Okay, honey, let's try tonight. Maybe you can get it up for me." Such a beginning puts both partners on the alert. Who will get the credit if the looked-for erection occurs? You know damn well who will get the blame if *she* fails.

If that same man and woman put aside the belief that showing love has to include intercourse, if they forget the *problem* and focus on the *process,* the evening can become one of intense pleasure and marvelous sharing. Who cares if he's erect or if she's ready to have an orgasm when they're both having a wonderfully intimate time together?

Ask yourself this question: "What is it I'm looking for when I share an hour or an evening with someone I love?" Are you really determined to count orgasms and erections? Or do you want to show your love, to express it in intimate ways that touch the inner core of the person most dear to you?

We've been told for years to take time to smell the daisies along the way. It isn't a new concept. We have, to some degree, taken the message to heart in our day-to-day living. I know a man who makes quite a thing about smelling flowers and watching sunsets, but he's goal-oriented when it comes to sex. He firmly believes that simultaneous orgasms are the epitome of good sex, and he works hard to achieve them. But far too often the ecstasy he expects never materializes. He expends so much energy on the goal, he has none left with which to enjoy the touching and kissing and caressing taking place along the way.

When I became a surrogate, I discovered that the way to extend sex pleasure with a partner is to become aware of each and every enjoyable act we share. I learned the beginning of sexual control through my first experiences of impotence during my class at the Center. I found I could hold off for longer periods. I was no longer controlled by my penis. That skill helps me when I work with a client.

I became multiorgasmic. Almost any man who wants to can learn the same skill without professional guidance. The book *Any Man Can,* by William Hartman and Marilyn Fithian—which includes detailed instructions on how to proceed in mastering the skill—was recently released by St. Martin's Press. I recommend it to any man who is interested in becoming multiorgasmic. But a word of warning. Most men have learned to have only one orgasm. There's no easy way to undo conditioning of such long standing. A man who decides to retrain himself in this way will have to spend time and energy to reach his goal.

This enhanced *physical* control, which can be learned, certainly does contribute to better sexual communication. But *psychological* control also increases understanding between a man and a woman. The two real villains for most men are goal orientation and time. Men fall victim to time pressure early in life. As boys, masturbating in bed or in the bathroom, they feel a need to rush. But there's no real need for hurrying when they mature. Lovemaking should be leisurely. You can't enjoy your partner if you rush to end sex as soon as it begins. So, whether you decide to try to become multiorgasmic or not, you can still learn to take your time.

When you have time to spend showing love, be as romantic as possible. Go out for a light dinner or bring home some take-out food and eat it by candlelight. Pour the wine into good glasses. When you move from food to lovemaking, do it slowly. Don't attack the genitals as if the rest of the body doesn't count. Tease each other until you both long for closer contact, for deeper penetration. If you learn to enjoy lovemaking, you can stretch it out for hours. This doesn't mean five or six hours of intercourse. I doubt anyone could find that enjoyable.

I dislike the term *foreplay*, because it implies a goal toward which a couple must move—that what takes place earlier isn't as important as the orgasm which follows. When you make love, every touch and caress should be a pleasure in itself. There should be no beginning, middle, or climax. There should be only an outpouring of affection, of wanting to be together, of holding and kissing and showing through every touch how much you care for each other.

What's the secret of being a great lover? It isn't devoting all your time and attention to another. Anyone who's had a relationship with a person who is too clinging knows how confining and oppressive that is. But be aware of your partner's needs and desires—and of your own— and don't always wait to do things until your wife or husband or lover asks you to. Above all, fulfill your partner's needs in ways that you, yourself, find most pleasurable.

When you begin to share love, don't be afraid to talk. Women often assume that men are mind readers. I assure you, they aren't. If you're a woman who loves to have her ear nibbled, say so. And don't be surprised if, next time, he's already forgotten. We men don't all have perfect memories. Especially when we're reacting to our own arousal, we aren't particularly alert. Give us a break. We need all the help we can get.

Inevitably, one particular position may feel very good and another less so. Yet a few minutes later (or maybe the next night or next week) those responses are reversed.

Both men and women need to remember that we change from day to day. Just because your partner didn't like something one time, don't write it off forever. Be willing to risk trying it again. Maybe this time it will give you both a pleasure you've never quite had before.

I've talked a lot about the sensate-focus exercises I do with my clients. They serve as passageways toward intimacy. Usually, we approach our partners only when we want sex. But sex is more enjoyable if we feel close all the time. Some of the exercises I've described in earlier chapters may never go beyond hugging and cuddling.

Maybe, when you first start to experience closeness, those exercises may seem too threatening. If you find yourself hesitating to get involved in caressing the nude back or upper body, try one of the following simple procedures, which can be done fully clothed.

Decide which of you will be active first. I suggest it be the person who wants to "do something." If you're that person, sit on the bed, back comfortably propped on a couple of pillows that rest on the headboard. Spread your legs and put a pillow on your lap. The room should be comfortably warm and semi-dark. You might have soft music playing in the background.

The receiving partner lies with head on the lap pillow, hands relaxed, and arms draped over your legs. Remove all jewelry, glasses, and contact lenses. Both of you close your eyes, take a few deep breaths, and relax.

Now put your hands under your partner's chin, cupping it gently. Pretend that you've just arrived on this planet and are encountering a human face for the first time. Explore this face with your fingers and hands, not with your eyes. Caress the chin and the jaw. Very slowly and gently, stroke your partner's nose and every nook and cranny of this face that lies before you. Touch the lips, feeling for contour, texture, and temperature. Move to the upper lip, working slowly over the cheekbones.

Let your hands wander over the eyes and up onto the forehead. Gently stroke the hairline and let your fingers play around the ears. Don't tickle. Make your touch firm enough to feel good, but remember, this isn't a massage. Don't knead the muscles. Stroke and caress the skin. Let yourself become aware of the texture of your partner's scalp beneath the hair. Take time to examine every facet of your partner's hair and face, as if you've never felt them before. Chances are, you haven't. We touch cheeks sometimes, and occasionally we stroke each other's hair, but that's about all we do.

Since you'll be feeling your partner's face from an up-side-down position, you might get lost. You may not be sure whether you're touching an eye or the lips. But don't let that disturb you. Just keep your touch gentle. Remember, you're doing it for your own enjoyment. Revel in this new experience. Both the giver and the receiver should take pleasure in the touching and in being touched.

Most of all, remember that there's no one "right" way to do this. You don't have to think about what feels best for your partner. Agree only that if your partner doesn't enjoy having some particular area stroked, you'll be told gently and then you'll move on to another place. When you're ready to stop, move your hands once more to the chin and cup it. Hold them there for a moment. Then reverse roles. The giver now becomes the receiver.

If you do this exercise with love and caring, slowly and tenderly, you may be amazed at the amount of intimacy you feel. You will both have shared in an experience of mutual trust and pleasure.

Another nonsexual exercise you might try involves the

feet. Again, I suggest that this contact be performed first by the person who wants to be active. This can be done in the living room or the den.

The receiver should remove shoes and socks and sit in a comfortable chair. The active partner fills a large plastic pan with warm water, places the tub on the floor at the receiving partner's feet, and sits beside it. Have a bar of soap, two bath towels, and some baby powder close by. The lights should be low, and some music you both enjoy should be playing softly.

Now you, as the giver, gently lift one foot of the receiver and place it in the pan of water. Use the soap as a lubricant to help your hands move around your partner's foot. Caress both the ankle and the top of the foot. Caress each toe as if you've never touched it before. Very possibly, you never have.

Gently run your fingers under the sole, being careful not to tickle. Explore every facet of that foot. After about five minutes, remove the foot from the water. Carefully towel it dry as it rests in your lap. Then put baby powder on it, gently rubbing and stroking it. With the towel still wrapped about it, put it on the floor. Then repeat the process with the other foot. The same need exists in this exercise as in the facial caress. Do it for your own pleasure. There is no goal, no performance level you must reach. Just enjoy each other. I have seen people reduced to tears by the emotion of this experience.

When you're finished, change places. Use fresh water and dry towels. Far too often we look upon feet with disdain. In this act of foot washing, in addition to establishing a kind of intimacy you probably never had before, you're telling your partner that you accept every part of his or her body. It will be a new experience for you both.

The same procedure can be used with hair grooming. This time, in another exercise involving mutual pleasuring, you alternate brushing each other's hair. If one partner is bald, caress the head or stroke it with a very soft brush. Once more, you're entering into an experience of stroking and closeness. There is no servant, no aggressor, no slave.

One other exercise I particularly enjoy is the sensuous shower. When you're both ready, heat up the bathroom and turn the water on to a slow drizzle. You're going to use water and soap only as a medium, a lubricant, not to get your partner clean.

If you're the giver, direct the water flow onto the receiver's back until it's thoroughly wet. Then, turning the water away, apply soap so your hands can move smoothly over your partner's body. Remember, this is a caress, not a massage.

Now you have the whole body available for touching. Let your hands glide over the neck, onto the shoulders, into the armpits, and down the back and sides. Caress the buttocks, the thighs, the inner and outer parts of the legs. Don't forget the knees and the toes. Then slowly work back up again, using only what soap and water is needed to provide lubrication. Don't take any more time on the genitals than you do on any other part of the body. Remember, the purpose of this exercise is to establish an intimacy and closeness and nurturing that isn't readily available in any other manner.

For this reason, don't make any demands if one of you gets aroused. This isn't supposed to be preparation for sex. Don't do anything overtly sexual. No one has ever died of sexual arousal. Just enjoy the arousal, experience it, be aware of how it feels and how it intensifies your reactions. Let your partner do the same. If you still feel sexy after you've both had the pleasure of caressing and being caressed, and the desire is mutual, you'll have all the time you need to do something more.

After you've finished caressing your partner's back and front, gently wash the soap off and reverse roles. Keep the water at a drizzle. A strong spray distracts and may even exhaust your hot-water supply. Allow about twenty minutes for each partner. Go slowly and, most of all, enjoy the stroking whether you're the giver or the receiver.

When the second partner is through being the giver, step out of the shower and gently dry each other off. Go into your bedroom and lie down. Be sure the phone is off the hook, the doors are locked, and the kids are with neighbors or relatives. For this intimate time, there are only two important people in the world—you and your partner.

Once more, powder or lightly oil each other's body. Despite the arousal you may feel, you may just want to cuddle and nap. But do what you wish, as long as it's mutual. You can always become more active when you awake and find you're still alone and together.

If you try any of these exercises and follow the simple rules (no overt sex, and no dominating of one person by the other), you may not feel as alone as you did before. If that happens, you'll know all's right between you and your mate. The warmth you thought was missing from your union will have suddenly returned.

And if it doesn't? Try again. Just don't abandon hope without giving intimacy a chance. Remember, if you, like Homer and Lila, can't seem to get on the same wavelength, you may need help. But don't let that dissuade you. Anything that revives the warmth and togetherness you felt when you first met is certainly worth some effort.

14

THE ESSENCE OF INTIMACY
A Surrogate's Stock-in-Trade

S urrogates are many things to their clients. They can assume various roles. They can be teacher, father, mother, husband, wife, lover, or confidant(e). But they must be aware of each role they assume so that, for whatever time is necessary, they fulfill the function needed.

While I am a member of a number of sex-therapy organizations and institutions and a working surrogate, I have not assumed the role of official spokesman for all surrogates. I have only made my own analysis of the role we play in therapy. My opinions are my own. Yet I suspect that many of my peers would at least nod approval to my conclusions.

We do get pleasure and satisfaction from our contact with clients, but that isn't why we're called in. We understand that we must always remain aware of the needs of our clients, alert for any clues that might help the therapist perform the required work. We don't necessarily know in advance what difficulties we might encounter. But when a problem surfaces, we're expected to maintain our perspective. We must be capable of recognizing when we've reached our goal, which is to explore the origins of our clients' difficulties. As sex surrogates, we open up channels of communication often unavailable in talk therapy or even in any other kind of human relationship.

When you consider how careful we must be to control our reactions so as not to harm our clients, you begin to understand how very sensitive the situation is. A spouse or lover is usually not prepared to deal with the emotions that surface. Loving partners can so easily make the wrong move and, in the process, set a person back by many years. Many problems that men and women finally bring to therapy would have been solved far more easily had they not been compounded by repeated, well-meaning attempts to make things right "next time."

When I meet a client for the first time, she is usually very uptight, estranged, lonely, suspicious, and confused. She keeps me at arm's length, both physically and mentally. But by the time we reach the last session, I've come to know her innermost thoughts and feelings, her most deeply hidden fantasies. In most cases, she has explored the responses of her body far more intensely and fully with me than she has with any other man. We've shared in her metamorphosis. I've become a part of her new life, as she has become a part of mine.

Trust and honesty are what allows a surrogate to become so intimate with a client in so short a time. When I work with a woman, I begin by showing her I can be trusted to do what I say. I won't rush her. I won't force her to do something against her will. The sensate-focused hand caressing and the hugging with which I start brings us in physical contact—but in a safe, nonsexual way.

We move together from that beginning, exposing our bodies, our sexual selves, and our minds equally. I believe very strongly that it is this combination of the three levels of relating that causes the magic to happen. Combined, they help my client see, maybe for the first time, that she is *sensual* even if, because of some problem, she doesn't feel *sexual.*

Trying to differentiate between sensuality and sexuality is sometimes difficult. For many people, the two words are synonymous. Often I find that only after a client has learned to integrate both qualities into her life is she able to differentiate between them.

I believe that most surrogates are very sensual people. Yet if you were to attend a meeting of IPSA, you would never know it. Only when the formal part of the meeting is over do we even discuss personal experiences or relate problems we're having with clients and ask for advice or assistance. Then we realize we aren't like every other group of business people who assemble. There is an energy in the room, an ambiance that's created by our common interest and our concern for others.

We certainly don't become involved in orgies or any other sexual activity, but there is a unique feeling of open sensuality and self-acceptance. And we accept one another. We've all reached a point in our growth where we're willing to speak openly about ourselves. We aren't playing games anymore. We dare to expose our weaknesses and to recognize our strengths. We're neither shamed by the former nor overly proud of the latter. We accept both as simple proof of our shared humanity. We accept one another as whole people with faults and special talents.

It was during my training that I came to understand the importance of dealing with the entire person. It's easy to assume that if people are having sexual problems, they need simple sex therapy. But sex therapy isn't enough when we're working with an individual who can't have orgasms, is a premature ejaculator, or is impotent. Those difficulties are only symptoms. Self-image is the critical factor. People who feel unworthy can never fully appreciate the unique beauty of their bodies or accept their right to happiness. They can't accept their sexuality because they can't accept themselves.

One of the early homework assignments I frequently give a client is to go out and buy something just for herself. Price isn't important. It can be of any value, from less than a dollar to the most she can afford. What matters is that it be something she's wanted and wouldn't ordinarily buy for herself.

It's interesting to me that she usually buys something for the house or the car if this purchase is made before we have our nude body-imaging session. After we've studied our bodies and she feels better about herself, she almost always opts for something more personal, like sexy underwear, a trip, a ticket to the theater, a bottle of perfume, or a day at the beach. This seems significant to me, for it's often the first time in her life she's acknowledged that she deserves pleasure.

As we move on in the sessions, I hear the anguish my clients feel because they have never experienced closeness and love. I'm aware of their distress when they can't enjoy sex or have an orgasm, when any contact with a penis gives them pain. I hear them speak of long-hidden fantasies and fears, which I never condemn.

I can understand their anger and bitterness when they speak of forced sex or cruel treatment from some man they thought they loved—or from a stranger who took advantage of their vulnerability. I listen to them voice hatred for fathers who mistreated or ignored them. And I'm receptive when they speak of their dissatisfaction with lovers and husbands. I share their frustrations with the world around them. I witness their desperation when they're qualified for a position at work but are pushed aside to make place for a male.

Most important of all, I'm also present during those times when they feel quiet, comfortable, and trusting. I'm with them—watching, listening, touching, and sharing—when they finally have their first orgasms. We talk about what happened. How did it feel? Why did it occur now and not before? We explore what they want in their future, and how they plan to keep the sensitivity they have now acquired.

I used to think I was honored with all this confidence because I, like them, had made many mistakes which I dared to admit. Like most men, I spent years hearing without listening, looking without seeing, touching without feeling. But now I realize that, though I share past errors with my clients, such sharing alone is not enough to arouse the confidence and trust given to me.

In a discussion with some of my fellow surrogates, I came to understand what it was that made us successful in this delicate task of probing into other people's souls for the roots of their unhappiness. It's our awareness of our own vulnerability. In our training we exposed ourselves to one another. We bared our weaknesses and were not rejected. I realize that some of us dared to go further than others in this uncovering of our inner selves. It appears that those of us who became most open are most successful and insightful with our clients.

I believe this process, this developing of total intimacy, forms the basis for the therapeutic solution to a client's emotional and sexual problems. It isn't the talk sessions, or the touching sessions, or the sex sessions alone that enable her to open up, to trust, to risk, and to relate to another human being, perhaps for the first time in her life. It's a combination of them all, mixed together in a way that's compatible with her needs.

Sex surrogates listen, touch, talk, and, if necessary, provide sexual instruction to fit the needs of their clients. They utilize the various processes and exercises they have learned during training so their clients will feel safe and willing to let go of the defenses with which they've isolated themselves from the world. With a surrogate partner beside them, they delve deep into themselves and learn to overcome the fears that kept them separated from love and affection.

When surrogates are successful, their clients adapt the lessons they learn so they become a part of their overall lifestyle. Their new self-acceptance and self-confidence transfers to every aspect of their living. These clients view themselves differently than they did when they first arrived at the therapist's door. They know their bodies as they've never known them before. They know what they like and don't like, both in sex and in daily living.

They dare, at last, to ask for what they want, since they no longer fear rejection. If they don't get agreement with their requests, they have learned how to negotiate. A new confidence emerges and becomes an integral part of their very essence. In business and social affairs, as in sex, they inspire respect and appreciation because they dare to be themselves.

How can surrogates contribute to such personal achievement? What powers do we have that we can work with hesitant, frightened individuals and guide them into self-acceptance and confidence?

First and foremost, we are aware of the people with whom we are working. We have learned to see outside ourselves and our own reactions. We have also learned to control our own lives. In the classes we attend, we learn to enjoy what we do and to recognize our enjoyment as acceptable. We learn to trust and to be trustworthy. We learn to approach and be approachable.

I realize that most people can't take time off and fly to one of the few big cities where Sexual Enrichment Classes are available. Nor can everyone afford sex therapy, even if they need it. But I'm confident that almost every individual can do something to increase the awareness of common humanity that dwells within us. I believe the first step is to recognize every person, male or female, as worthy and deserving of happiness. For some men, that means looking at women in a totally new way, because many males today still consider women different—and inferior.

I was fortunate. I never had to overcome that prejudice. All my life I've been influenced by women. When I became a surrogate, I was privileged to probe deeper into the minds and the sexuality of my clients than most men ever can. I learned to listen. I discovered that, though women might use different words than those I was accustomed to hearing from men, they had much the same things to tell me. I also learned that as different as they appeared to be at first glance, women were actually far more like me than not.

Early in life, I learned to admire the courage with which women faced a world that put them down and paid them less money than men. I saw the many insidious ways in which women were denigrated in our society, and I appreciated the vigor with which so many maintained their self-respect despite all the insults that were hurled at them in the media, the business world, and in their own homes.

When I became a surrogate, I developed a great respect for every woman who came to me for help. They all deserved admiration. True, they had problems, but they were willing to do something to solve them. They were willing to take risks, and they had real courage, for they dared to come to strangers for help in a most intimate area of their lives.

They were courageous, too. They were willing to let themselves trust someone, completely and without reservation. This is very difficult for *anyone* to do. It is especially hard for someone who has already been hurt, as most of my clients have been, by men who seemed selfish and cruel.

They had true humility. They were able to put aside false pride. They were willing to pay money (in most cases hard-earned) in order to find solutions to their problems. To do this, they had to decide that they were deserving of all the effort, time, and money they might have to expend. They came for help, not necessarily to make things easier for someone else but to improve their own lives, which they felt were in a shambles.

Surrogates share with the therapist the responsibility of leading clients to heal themselves. We're expected to move at a speed that's comfortable for them. We do not operate under a set of rigid rules, yet there is one "must" we cannot forget. We *must* keep our clients aware of the here and now. We can't let them make giant leaps from what is happening *now* to what they believe is supposed to follow.

Often, a client of mine assumes that if she has sex in a certain way, with a man who has a certain size penis, or who can last for a certain length of time, she should then have an orgasm. When her expectations aren't fulfilled, she's convinced that something is wrong with her. She decides she's unskilled or incapable as a person. If she can't face her own culpability, then she may conclude the man is at fault. He's unskilled, unfeeling, or a premature ejaculator.

Only after she works with me for some time does she

begin to concentrate her attention on the pleasure she receives in the process of touching, caressing, and loving. She forgets then to think about the orgasm she wants. She lets herself enjoy the warm affection we're sharing. When that occurs, she is, at last, living in the here and now.

A new concept? Of course not. We've all been told the value of being aware of the present and the hazards of expending too much energy on what was or might be. But how are we to keep ourselves from regretting the past or anticipating the future to the detriment of what's happening to us now?

My experience leads me to believe that in sex we have the key. If we can learn to enjoy every touch, closeness, and intimacy with a partner in sex, we can project that ability into other aspects of our lives.

If an alien from another galaxy landed on this planet, he might be hard-pressed to understand what we meant by the word *sex*. The dictionary would provide such definitions as "either of two divisions of organisms distinguished respectively as male or female" or "to identify the gender of . . ." or, finally, "the sphere of interpersonal behavior, especially between male and female, directly associated with, leading up to, substituting for, or resulting from genital union." But the definitions would not convey the emotions that human sexuality evokes.

Similarly, the definitions of the word *intimate* would provide little insight. Neither "marked by warm friendship developing through long association," "suggesting informal warmth or privacy," or "of a very personal or private nature" can adequately convey the trust and vulnerability that is part and parcel of true intimacy. This alien would still not have a clear picture of the concepts involved. If he were told that a *sex act* was the insertion of one penis into one vagina, he would probably accept that definition without question. But, again, the emotions that accompany that act would be missing.

With the exception of some lifelong celibate, I don't believe there's any reader who would benefit from such a lesson. *Sex* and *intimacy* are both terms that contain many subtle shades of meaning. To be successful in sexual communication, men and women need to understand more than superficial definitions. They need to understand and feel affection for each other. They need to want to get and to give pleasure.

I think it's important to understand that no one is going to get every need met all of the time. In a good relationship, such as a happy marriage or a successful living-together arrangement, there are three possible problem areas—his, hers, and theirs. And these areas are constantly changing as the individuals change. There are bound to be times when one partner has real needs of a sexual nature that clash with a different kind of need in the other.

In a close relationship where both partners are committed to making it work, each one must be willing to give 100 percent and maybe, at times at least, take only 50 percent. This builds a vast reserve on which both may draw when their needs are not immediately met. If one person desires touching, or caring, or affection, or something explicitly sexual, and the other has a need to be alone, it should be possible for the one who wants affection to control that need until it can be fulfilled. Despite fables to the contrary, no one has ever died from temporary lack of sex. If the delay becomes unbearable, the needy partner can always resort to masturbation or a cold shower.

If both partners care about each other and are truly concerned for each other's welfare, they can usually work out some adjustments so that their unbalanced cycles begin to meet. In such a situation, the concept of negotiation is most important. Frequently, there is a middle ground that will satisfy both partners, even if only temporarily. One solution I have found useful is for both partners to have a special night set aside each week which is designated as "My Night." One week one partner has the privilege of choosing what is to happen, the next week the other is in charge.

If a man and woman have been together for some time, truly respect each other, and have developed a sense of intimacy, these "My Nights" will not be offensive. They can even embellish the idea. Maybe one night a year they can have an "Off-the-Wall Night" in which they do something different and unusual just to spice up their relationship. Such an infusion of new ideas is often all that's needed to bring freshness and a feeling of specialness into a relationship, especially one of long standing. However, if the inability to communicate and be intimate becomes habitual, the couple needs to examine the problem together, and the less-responsive partner should seek help—most probably of a professional nature.

One major difference between the relationship of a surrogate and client and a successful marriage or love union is that surrogates know from the start that their interaction with a client will be of limited duration. From the very first, we talk about how our sessions together will end. This influences us to make good use of our time.

Another critical quality of surrogate-client relationships is that we aim to help our clients transfer what they learn with us to partners they will choose or to a partner they already have. If all we needed to teach them was how to have sex—whether better or just more—we could accomplish our goal in about an hour. But we aim higher. We try to help our clients experience intimacy so that they'll seek it with others. We guide them into ways that will allow them to feel completely comfortable with other human beings. We teach them how to avoid condemning themselves for past mistakes and others for unintentional errors. We help them overcome demands that they perform in some predetermined manner. And most of all, we teach them to enjoy the process through which they achieve their sexual goals.

If a client doesn't learn to trust me within a few weeks of our first meeting, she may sever our connection, feeling despair and a sense of rejection, certain that somehow she is responsible for the failure. This makes it imperative that I establish trust and intimacy quickly. If I can't do that, I must at least convince her that if we are unable to reach this kind of closeness, no one is to blame.

During our times together, we expose our vulnerabilities and our fears. We're careful, however, never to exploit each other's mistakes or sensitivities. Yet we are not always serious. We have fun, too. In the fifteen to thirty weeks we're together, we go through, in microcosm, the entire process of meeting, making plans, dreaming, realizing progress, and developing a relationship that matters to us both.

Eventually, we part, leaving each other for good. This, too, is what often happens in human relationships. But we don't separate in anger or despair. We're secure in the realization that we've profited by knowing each other. Each has left imprints on the other that will benefit us both for the rest of our lives.

We come together in trust. Sometimes we have sex, sometimes we don't. Either way, we put aside the defenses with which we usually shield ourselves from contact with others. We dare this because we've agreed at the start that we will not separate without a final farewell. If our relationship doesn't become intimate, we still have that closing session that allows us to discuss the difficulties we encountered. If we grew to love each other, we go our separate ways only after having expressed our thankfulness at having met. I know my clients are often helped by the hours they've spent with me. But I, too, come away from each encounter with a feeling of having grown.

Most of us have experienced the satisfaction of knowing that a partner is enjoying what we are doing. However, if you caress your partner and begin to realize you're not giving the pleasure you meant to, you, yourself, can no longer enjoy what you're doing. That seems obvious. But look at the situation from another point of view as well. Put yourself in the place of the receiver. If you know your partner does not enjoy giving you the caresses you receive, if you're sure they're provided only because you've asked for them, you can't relax and enjoy yourself, either.

This is the basic reason for the sensate-focus exercises. They are done to teach the client to *take* pleasure so that what is done can be enjoyed by both partners. It's a circular, reciprocal situation. Both must enjoy what is being done. Otherwise, neither one can really relax and take pleasure in what is happening.

Therefore, when you begin to experiment with touching, don't do anything you don't truly want to. Look for a way to take pleasure in all your actions. When you hug or caress or touch, concentrate on your own enjoyment. Be aware that you like what you're doing. Only then will you be able to give pleasure. Only when you and your partner both enjoy what you do will an intimacy develop which can open the door to new feelings of freedom, love, and self-acceptance.

We relive our hurts and pains and, through sharing and love, find healing. We expose our needs and desires, and find them reflected in the longings of our partners.

We learn to show love because we feel it, to embrace because we want to have our partner near us, to caress because touching gives us pleasure. And because we trust our partners to feel as we do, we can take pleasure in being loved, embraced, and caressed.

This, then, is reaching intimacy.